ABC NEWSROOM

Shigeru Yamane
Kathleen Yamane

KINSEIDO

Kinseido Publishing Co., Ltd.
3-21 Kanda Jimbo-cho, Chiyoda-ku,
Tokyo 101-0051, Japan

First published 2023 by Kinseido Publishing Co., Ltd.

Cover design: Haruka Ito
Text design: DAITECH co., ltd.

Video Material: Copyright © 2022 ABC, Inc.

音声ファイル無料ダウンロード

https://www.kinsei-do.co.jp/download/4171

この教科書で DL 00 の表示がある箇所の音声は、上記 URL または QR コードにて無料でダウンロードできます。自習用音声としてご活用ください。

- ▶ PC からのダウンロードをお勧めします。スマートフォンなどでダウンロードされる場合は、**ダウンロード前に「解凍アプリ」をインストール**してください。
- ▶ URL は、**検索ボックスではなくアドレスバー (URL 表示欄)** に入力してください。
- ▶ お使いのネットワーク環境によっては、ダウンロードできない場合があります。

CD 00 左記の表示がある箇所の音声は、教室用 CD（Class Audio CD）に収録されています。

Foreword

World News Tonight, the flagship news program of the American Broadcast Company, is enjoyed by millions of Americans each evening at 6:30. Watching it together was part of my family's daily routine when I was growing up in New York. With its reputation for balanced, fair reporting by a news team who take a personalized look at what's happening around the world, the show is consistently at the top of the evening news ratings.

Since the publication of this textbook series began more than three decades ago, the popular newscasts have become part of the learning experience of tens of thousands of Japanese students, as well. This text is the first one in our new series, incorporating a number of changes that we feel will enhance the learning experience. As always, we have made a great effort to select stories that are not only important but will also make young adults think a little bit harder about the world outside of Japan. This edition includes a stimulating cross section of topics, from the discovery of a sunken ship in Antarctica to the controversial "Don't Say Gay" bill in Florida. Students will meet inspiring heroes like the newest Supreme Court Justice, the "Marathon Mom" and the eight-year-old author of a popular Christmas story. These news stories will take you all across the U.S. and beyond, from the Galapagos Islands to the Ukraine and on Holocaust Remembrance Day, to the former concentration camp at Auschwitz. We feel certain that you will find them all to be as fascinating as we do.

Back in 1987, no one associated with this ABC World News textbook project imagined that the series would have such longevity and touch the lives of so many students. We believe that adopting authentic broadcast news materials for classroom use is a powerful way to build English skills while also helping students to become more knowledgeable about world affairs and to develop the critical thinking skills necessary for all young people in today's increasingly interconnected world. Many of our students also tell us that using the text was good preparation for the TOEFL and TOEIC exams and for job interviews.

To the students using *ABC NEWSROOM*, remember that the skills that you develop using this book can be applied to other news shows, even when the course is over. We sincerely hope that you will challenge yourselves to become more aware of world events and be inspired to follow the news more closely. Happy studying!

January, 2023

Kathleen Yamane
Shigeru Yamane

まえがき

近年，日常生活における情報源としてインターネットの活用がますます盛んになってきている。このような高度な情報化社会では，不正確な情報や見方の偏った情報も多くあふれている。学生諸君は，何が本当に自分に役立つ正しい情報か，情報の「質」を見極める能力を身につける必要があるのではないだろうか。

一般的に，テレビニュースからの情報は信頼性が高いといわれている。本書はアメリカの３大ネットワーク（ABC，CBS，NBC）の一つである，ABC放送からのテレビニュース番組を録画し，それを文字化した上で，テキスト用に編集したものである。収録したニュースは米国東部標準時間夕方６時30分から毎日放送されているABC放送の看板ニュース番組*World News Tonight with David Muir*である。

1948年に始まり，長い歴史を誇るこのABC放送のニュース番組は，ピーター・ジェニングズなど，多くの人気キャスターを生み出してきた。2014年にディビッド・ミューアがアンカーパーソンに抜擢され，さらに人気が高まった。2015年３月には「アメリカで最も多く視聴されている夕方のニュース番組」となり，アメリカ国内でも絶大な人気を保ちながら，質の高い情報を毎日提供し続けている。

今回も，そのABC放送の看板番組の中から，大学生が学ぶにふさわしい多種多様なニュースを15本厳選し，収録することができた。アメリカ国内のニュースだけではなく，「107年前の探検船が見つかる」や「ガラパゴス島の生態系を守る」など，世界のニュースも含まれている。「『ゲイと言ってはいけない法』が成立」，「銃乱射事件の遺族と銃メーカーが和解」など，本書で取り上げた現在の社会が抱えるさまざまなトピックを学ぶことを通じて，学生諸君にはニュースの理解を深めながら，自分の意見も持ってもらいたい。また，身近で親しみやすい話題としては，「ラブランドからのバレンタインカード」，考えさせる話題としては，「アウシュビッツを訪れた生存者たち」など多く収録した。

ニュースを収録した映像は，専用のウェブサイトplus+Media上でストリーミング視聴することができる。ぜひ，学生諸君にはこの映像を繰り返し見てもらいたい。アメリカの人々が家庭で毎日見ている良質のニュース番組に触れ，信頼できる情報をもとに英語を学んでもらいたい。

本シリーズは1987年に*TV News from the U.S.A.*として始まった。その後，1999年から*ABC World News*として20年間毎年出版され続けた。また2019年には，さまざまな箇所に改良を加え，*Broadcast: ABC WORLD NEWS TONIGHT*と書名を変更し生まれ変わった。さらに今回は，音声の充実を図ると共に，*ABC NEWSROOM*と書名を一新した。アメリカABC放送のニュースを利用した本シリーズは，今回で通算30冊目になり，お陰様で長年にわたり毎回たいへん好評を頂いている。2010年度には外国語教育メディア学会（LET）から，本教材の開発に対して，LET学会賞の「教材開発賞」を受賞する栄誉を頂いた。今後もさらにより良い教材開発の努力を続けていきたい。

最後になったが，テキスト作成に際して毎回大変お世話になっている金星堂のみなさん，今回もこころよく版権を許可してくださったアメリカABC放送に心から感謝の意を表したい。

2023年1月

山根　繁
Kathleen Yamane

Table of Contents

Volunteers in Loveland

The Gist
- What happens each year in Loveland, Colorado around Valentine's Day?
- Who handles the work?

Before You Watch the News — *Warm-up Exercises*

A Vocabulary Check: Choose the correct definition for each of the words below.

DL 02 CD1-02

1. swell ( )
2. namesake ( )
3. fulfill ( )
4. labor of love ( )
5. pass away ( )

a. to achieve; to bring something to completion
b. to expand or grow
c. to die
d. rewarding work done voluntarily
e. a person or thing named after someone or something else

B Fill in the blanks with appropriate expressions from the Vocabulary Check above. Change the word forms where necessary.

1. The river ( ) after days of heavy rain, threatening another flood.
2. Mary's adorable ( ) has the same blue eyes as her grandmother.
3. Greg's father ( ) last month following a long illness.
4. At the age of 50, Tohru finally ( ) his dream of climbing Mt. Fuji.
5. For Kelly, caring for stray animals is a ( ).

Focus on the News Story

L. Davis: Finally, tonight, it has a population of about 77,000 people, but around Valentine's Day, the mail in Loveland, Colorado swells to more than 200,000, 1. ________________________ in need of a special touch.

Here in the city of Loveland, Colorado, love is in the air, and the streets, and the people.

Volunteer 1: It's called love. L-o-v-e.

L. Davis: I guess you could say it's the kind of place where people wear their hearts on their sleeves and glasses and heads. Living up to their namesake, 2. ________________________, volunteers in Loveland have been stamping and mailing out hundreds of thousands of Valentines.

Volunteer 2: People send their cards 3. ________________________ right here to be hand-stamped by our volunteers.

L. Davis: They typically receive 200,000 requests to remail Valentine cards. This year, orders poured into the sweetheart city from all 50 states and 110 countries. Fulfilling the requests is a labor of love for some 200 volunteers, adding a special verse and postmark from Valentine Station to each love letter. So popular, Beverly Mortimer had to wait almost 15 years to be called off the waiting list. Joan and Joyce have been volunteering here 4. ________________________.

Volunteer 1: I have to take them a grain of—with a grain of salt, but a margarita on the side.

L. Davis: And this year, the tradition meant even more to Joan.

Volunteer 1: My husband and I moved up here in Loveland. We loved it up here. And then he passed away, and I started doing Valentines. And I like volunteering, and it's the best therapy [5.] ____________________ ____________________.

Volunteers: Happy Valentine's Day!

L. Davis: Happy Valentine's Day, everybody. Thanks so much for watching. David Muir, right back here tomorrow. I'm Linsey Davis. Have a great night.

Notes

- L.2 **Loveland** 「ラブランド〈コロラド州の州都デンバーの北に位置する都市〉」
- L.4 **in need of a special touch** 「特別な仕上げが必要な〈ラブランド市の消印を押したり，ことばを添えたりすること〉」
- L.5 **in the air** 「街中に漂っている；街中が（愛に）満ちている」
- L.9 **Living up to ~** 「（期待）に応えて」
- L.12 **Valentines** 「バレンタイン・カード〈2月14日に大切な人に贈るカード〉」
- L.16 **sweetheart city** 「愛の街」
- L.18 **verse** 「ことば」
- L.20 **to be called off the waiting list** 「キャンセル待ちのリストから外される〈ボランティアに採用される〉」
- L.22 **I have to ... a margarita on the side.** 「（手紙がたくさん来てボランティアは大変だけど）気楽に考えてマルガリータでもそばに置いておくわ；やることはたくさんあるけれども，楽しく軽やかにやっていきましょう〈もともと take ~ with a grain of salt は「～を話半分に聞く」という意味。them はたくさんの手紙を指すものと思われる。また，マルガリータを飲むときには，グラスの縁に塩をつけるのが一般的な習慣で，ボランティア仲間と冗談を言い合っている〉」

After You Watch the News — *Exercises*

A Listen to the news story and fill in the blanks in the text.

CD1-03 [Normal] CD1-04 [Slow]

B **T/F Questions:** Mark the following sentences true (T) or false (F) according to the information in the news story.

(   ) **1.** The population of Loveland swells dramatically every year around Valentine's Day.
(   ) **2.** Volunteers remail letters that are sent to Loveland.
(   ) **3.** Some of the volunteers come from overseas.
(   ) **4.** Loveland has been doing Valentines for more than 75 years.
(   ) **5.** Volunteering is so popular that there is a waiting list.
(   ) **6.** One woman moved to Loveland to begin volunteering when her husband died.

C Translate the following Japanese into English. Then listen to the CD and practice the conversation with your partner.

DL 03 CD1-05

A: 1. ____
______________________?

B: Of course I am! I had to wait for years to be called off the waiting list, so I plan to do this forever.

A: Me, too! 2. ______________________________. What could be better than that?

B: It's truly a labor of love.

A: It is! And volunteering has been a great way to make new friends.

B: 3. ____.

A: Come on, let's go sign up.

1. あなたは今年もバレンタインデーのボランティアをするつもりですか。
2. 私たちは愛を広める手助けをしているのです。
3. それ(ボランティア)は，私たちと世界中の何千人もの人々をつないでくれます。

D Summary Practice: Fill in the blanks with suitable words beginning with the letters indicated. Then listen to the CD and check your answers.

DL 04 CD1-06

What's in a name? (1. **L**) is in the news again, as it is every year at this time. For (2. **s**)-(3. **s**) years now, this town has been sending out (4. **V**) cards with a special (5. **v**) and a Loveland (6. **p**). A team of (7. **t**) (8. **h**) enthusiastic (9. **v**) stamps and sends out cards that have been sent to Loveland from all (10. **f**) states and 110 foreign (11. **c**). Although they normally have 200,000 (12. **o**) to fill, for the volunteers, it is a (13. **l**) of (14. **l**). In fact, some of them have been volunteering for (15. **d**). They can imagine the joy of the lucky people who (16. **r**) Valentine messages from their (17. **s**), sent from this special town in (18. **C**). How lovely is that?

E Discussion: Share your ideas and opinions with your classmates.

1. Loveland has branded itself as the "sweetheart city," creating a Valentine's Day tradition around its name. Work in a group and brainstorm other cities that have found original branding strategies connected to their names. (Example: Obama City in Fukui Prefecture)

2. How is Valentine's Day celebrated in Japan? See if you can find information about Valentine's Day traditions in other parts of the world. Share your findings with the class.

Commemorating Juneteenth

The Gist
- What is Juneteenth?
- How is it being celebrated around the U.S.?

Before You Watch the News — *Warm-up Exercises*

A **Vocabulary Check:** Choose the correct definition for each of the words below.

DL 05 CD1-07

1. commemorate ( ) a. opposition; refusal to accept
2. peers ( ) b. people of the same age or group
3. federal ( ) c. relating to the central government
4. resistance ( ) d. to publicly support
5. advocate (v.) ( ) e. to remember and show respect for someone or something

B Fill in the blanks with appropriate expressions from the Vocabulary Check above. Change the word forms where necessary.

1. People who (　　　　) same sex marriage should join today's march.
2. Gina has to start paying both (　　　　) and state taxes after graduating.
3. The statue near the café (　　　　) the town's 100-year anniversary.
4. Craig is respected by all of his (　　　　). I'll be happy to write a letter of recommendation for him.
5. Although they had expected a strong fight, the legal team met little (　　　　) to their proposed strategy.

Focus on the News Story

L. Davis: Tonight, Americans across the country are commemorating Juneteenth, the national holiday marking the day the last enslaved people in Texas first learned that they were free. There were celebrations and events across the country, a large crowd turning out for a parade and celebration in Milwaukee. Here's ABC's Zachary Kiesch.

Z. Kiesch: Tonight, Juneteenth, a day honoring America's march towards racial equality, [1.] ______________________________ ____________.

Pedestrian: It just makes us so happy to be able to be around our peers and to see all these beautiful black people here and [2.] ____________ ______________________________.

Z. Kiesch: The national holiday acknowledges the long-fought freedom for black Americans living in chattel slavery. In 1865, two and a half years after the Emancipation Proclamation, federal troops informed black enslaved people in Galveston, Texas that they were free.

And this weekend, [3.] ______________________________.
In Buffalo, a mark of the continued fight, the community coming together after 10 black lives were recently taken. In Ft. Worth, 95-year-old Opal Lee, a leading advocate of the holiday and often referred to [4.] ______________________________,

showing black joy is an act of resistance. Her tradition, a two-and-a-half-mile walk, symbolic of the additional time it took for those in Galveston.

O. Lee, Juneteenth activist: I'm advocating that we celebrate freedom from the 19th of June to the 4th of July.

Z. Kiesch: Juneteenth will be observed tomorrow [5.] ______________________________ ____________. That said, several states still do not acknowledge the day as a legal holiday.

Notes

- **L.2 Juneteenth** 「ジューンティーンス；奴隷解放記念日〈1865年6月19日に，テキサス州に到着した北軍によって，奴隷が解放されたことにちなむ記念日（毎年6月19日）。1863年には「奴隷解放宣言」が発令されたものの，南部の多くの地域では奴隷制が続き，テキサス州は最後まで奴隷解放に抵抗していた。June と nineteenth の混成語〉」
- **L.5 Milwaukee** 「ミルウォーキー〈ウィスコンシン州南東部，ミシガン湖に臨む同州最大の都市〉」
- **L.10 be able to be around ~** 「～と（こうやって）一緒にいられること」
- **L.14 chattel slavery** 「奴隷；動産奴隷制度〈奴隷として所有された人や奴隷制度を指す。奴隷の子や孫も自動的に奴隷とされる制度で，動産として売買の対象とされた〉」
- **L.15 the Emancipation Proclamation** 「奴隷解放宣言〈第16代大統領エイブラハム・リンカーン（Abraham Lincoln）により1863年に公布された〉」
- **L.16 Galveston** 「ガルベストン〈テキサス州南東部に位置する都市〉」
- **L.18 Buffalo** 「バッファロー〈ニューヨーク州西部，エリー湖に臨む港市。奴隷解放運動時代，南部から脱出した黒人奴隷たちは，バッファローを経由してフェリーでカナダへ逃亡して自由の身となった。また，2022年5月14日，同市のスーパーで男が銃を乱射し，10人が死亡した。黒人を意図的に狙った可能性が指摘されている〉」
- **L.19 Ft. Worth** 「フォートワース〈= Fort Worth テキサス州北部に位置する都市〉」
- **L.22 a two-and-a-half-mile walk** 「2.5マイルの歩行〈2016年，リーさんはテキサス州からワシントンD.C.まで，ジューンティーンスの連邦祝日化を訴えながら毎日2.5マイルずつ歩いた。この2.5マイルは，テキサス州で奴隷解放を知らされたのが1863年の奴隷解放宣言から2年半かかったことを象徴している〉」
- **L.28 That said** 「とは言え；そうは言っても」

Background of the News

2021年6月17日，バイデン大統領は6月19日を連邦祝日（national holiday）とする法案に署名した。この日は，最後まで奴隷制度が続いていたテキサス州で黒人奴隷制度の廃止が告げられたことから「奴隷解放記念日」とされている。1863年に公布されたリンカーン大統領による奴隷解放宣言以降も，特に南部の州では奴隷制が続いていた。1865年に北軍のゴードン・グレンジャー将軍がテキサス州ガルベストンに入り，“The people of Texas are informed that, in accordance with a Proclamation from the Executive of the United States, all slaves are free”と奴隷解放を宣言した。

連邦祝日は，この日を加えて年間11日あるが，米国で連邦の祝日が新たに設けられたのは，1983年に公民権運動指導者マーティン・ルーサー・キング牧師の誕生日を祝日と定めたキング牧師記念日（Martin Luther King Jr. Day）以来，38年ぶりとなった。連邦祝日を祝日と定めるかは州によって異なるものの，2022年の同日には各地で人種的平等（racial equality）を訴えるデモ行進，パレード，祝典（celebration）が催された。

2020年5月25日，ミネソタ州のミネアポリスで黒人男性のジョージ・フロイドさんが白人警官に首を圧迫されて死亡した事件を機に，黒人差別に抗議する「ブラック・ライブズ・マター」（Black Lives Matter: BLM）運動が全米に広がり，この日を連邦の祝日にするよう求める声が高まっていた。ジューンティーンスを連邦の祝日とすることで，米国の歴史における奴隷解放の意義を再認識し，黒人に対する人種差別といった根強い問題の解消に向けて機運を高める狙いがあるといわれている。

After You Watch the News　*Exercises*

A Listen to the news story and fill in the blanks in the text.

CD1-08 [Normal]　CD1-09 [Slow]

B **T/F Questions:** Mark the following sentences true (T) or false (F) according to the information in the news story.

( ) **1.** Juneteenth celebrations take place in many cities in the U.S.
( ) **2.** The Emancipation Proclamation officially freed black Americans from slavery in 1865.
( ) **3.** Juneteenth has been celebrated every year since 1865.
( ) **4.** Black slaves in Galveston did not know they had gained their freedom for over two years.
( ) **5.** Opal Lee does a symbolic two-and-a-half mile walk every year.
( ) **6.** Juneteenth is a legal holiday in every American state.

C Translate the following Japanese into English. Then listen to the CD and practice the conversation with your partner.

DL 06 CD1-10

A: Who is this Opal Lee everyone is talking about?
B: You really don't know? **1.** ______________________________.
A: Why?
B: Well, **2.** ______________________________. She even wants to get it extended to the 4th of July!
A: Wait a minute—**3.** ______________________________?
B: That's Opal all right! She's a real symbol of black joy.
A: I've got to meet that woman! Hey—let's join her walk next week.
B: Great idea!

1. 彼女はジューンティーンスの祖母と呼ばれています。
2. 彼女はジューンティーンスの主要な提唱者です。
3. 彼女が2.5マイルのウォーキングの伝統を始めた女性ですか。

D **Summary Practice:** Fill in the blanks with suitable words beginning with the letters indicated. Then listen to the CD and check your answers.

DL 07 CD1-11

Black Americans all across the country are celebrating (1. **J**) this week with (2. **c**), (3. **p**) and other (4. **e**). Although it is still not recognized as a (5. **l**) holiday in some states, June (6. **n**) has an important significance for black Americans, as it (7. **m**) the day when the last (8. **e**) blacks in (9. **G**), (10. **T**) finally learned that they had won their long-fought (11. **f**). However, it was a full two-and-a-half years after the (12. **E**) (13. **P**) that they learned from (14. **f**) (15. **t**) that they were free. In (16. **B**) this year, the day is a reminder that the (17. **f**) is not over, as the community mourns the loss of 10 black (18. **l**). Still, they will be joining people across the country showing pride in their black (19. **c**) and (20. **h**) on this important day.

E **Discussion:** Share your ideas and opinions with your classmates.

1. How much do you know about the slave trade that brought Africans to the southern states starting back in the 16th century? Do an internet search to learn more about the Atlantic Triangle. How many slaves were brought to America? What were conditions like for them?
2. Try to find more information about ways in which African Americans celebrate Juneteenth. Share your findings with your classmates.

Penguin at Arizona Aquarium

The Gist
- What is special about Rosie the Penguin?
- How is she inspiring children with special needs?

Before You Watch the News — *Warm-up Exercises*

A Vocabulary Check: Choose the correct definition for each of the words below.

DL 08 CD1-12

1. misaligned ( )
2. flap ( )
3. shuffle ( )
4. adapt ( )
5. cherish ( )

a. to adjust or modify
b. to move up and down or back and forth; to flutter
c. crooked; uneven
d. to treasure
e. to walk with short, slow steps

B Fill in the blanks with appropriate expressions from the Vocabulary Check above. Change the word forms where necessary.

1. As part of their wedding vows, the new couple promised to ( ) each other forever.
2. After his fall, Grandpa could only ( ) slowly through the house.
3. If the tray is ( ), the printer will not work properly.
4. Look! The baby bird is ( ) his wings. He might be trying to fly.
5. Jenny ( ) quickly to the new lifestyle when she moved to Italy.

Focus on the News Story

D. Muir: Finally, Rosie the Penguin.

Tonight, the team at OdySea Aquarium in Scottsdale, Arizona. They want you to meet Rosie the Penguin and the difference she's making in the lives of children. It's "America Strong."

1. ______________________________, the team began to notice Rosie was healthy, but could not sit up on her own. Her feet, misaligned, they say. So the aquarium had an idea. To strengthen Rosie and her leg muscles, the animal care team constructing this sling out of a baby onesie, and some elastic straps.

Zookeeper: Hi, Rosie girl.

D. Muir: Rosie, 2. ______________________________.

Zookeeper: Oh, girl.

D. Muir: Then, slowly, bearing weight on her legs.

Zookeeper: Oh, there you go. Easy.

D. Muir: 3. ______________________________, flapping her wings, slowly walking, baby steps.

Zookeeper: That's it. Good job.

D. Muir: And then look at Rosie go, walking right beside them.

Zookeeper: You're doing it.

D. Muir: Eventually [4.] ____ __________. Now Rosie, meeting children with their own challenges.

Child 1: Wow.

D. Muir: These children, all with special needs, connecting with Rosie.

Zookeeper: You can see her very unique shuffle and how she has learned to adapt.

D. Muir: Olivia walking right beside Rosie, then hugging her dad.

Father: Yeah, was that awesome?

Child 2: Hi, David.

D. Muir: The children on Rosie:

Child 2: I felt like meeting Rosie was really inspiring.

Child 3: Hi, David.

D. Muir: Celeste, too.

Child 3: I love her.

D. Muir: And Edgar making a "thank you" for the team at the aquarium.

C. Mann, clinical director: Hi, David.

D. Muir: Chantel Mann, the clinical director.

C. Mann: I know that it's a memory that our families are going to cherish forever.

D. Muir: No question. 5. ________________________________ and, of course, the children. I'll see you tomorrow. Good night.

Notes

- L.2 **OdySea Aquarium** 「オディシー水族館〈6,000 匹以上の生き物を飼育するアリゾナ州最大の水族館〉」
- L.2 **Scottsdale** 「スコッツデール〈アリゾナ州中部の都市〉」
- L.4 **America Strong** 「アメリカ・ストロング〈「強くあれ，アメリカ」という心温まるニュース，アメリカを元気にしてくれるニュースを紹介するコーナー〉」
- L.9 **baby onesie** 「赤ちゃん用ロンパース〈幼児用の上下一体型の服〉」
- L.13 **bearing weight on ~** 「～に体重をかける」
- L.23 **with special needs** 「援助を必要とする；障がいを抱える」
- L.29 **The children on Rosie:** 「ロージーについて子どもたちから寄せられた声［感想］」
- L.36 **clinical director** 「クリニカル・ディレクター；臨床研究の責任者」

After You Watch the News — *Exercises*

A Listen to the news story and fill in the blanks in the text.

B **T/F Questions:** Mark the following sentences true (T) or false (F) according to the information in the news story.

( ) **1.** The aquarium staff first noticed that Rosie had some problems when she was two years old.

( ) **2.** The animal care team had to teach Rosie to sit up on her own before they could teach her to walk.

( ) **3.** Rosie needed surgery in order to correct her misaligned feet.

( ) **4.** The children with special needs feel a loving connection to Rosie.

( ) **5.** Since her special training, Rosie is now able to walk just like the other penguins.

( ) **6.** The clinical director believes that the special needs children who visit Rosie will cherish the memory forever.

C Translate the following Japanese into English. Then listen to the CD and practice the conversation with your partner. DL 09 CD1-15

A: Where are you going for your family trip this summer, Kate?

B: To Scottsdale, in Arizona. We're planning to visit OdySea Aquarium.

A: 1. ____

____________? There's a terrific one right here in Chicago.

B: Tommy saw a video about Rosie the Penguin and he wants to meet her.

A: I saw something about Rosie on the news! 2. ______________________________

____

__________________, right?

B: That's right! 3. ____

______________________________.

A: What a great memory that will be, Kate! Have a nice trip.

1. どうして水族館に行くためだけに，そんなに遠くまでドライブするのですか。
2. 水族館のスタッフは，赤ちゃん用のロンパースで作ったスリングを使って，ロージーが歩けるように手伝ったのですよね。
3. 彼ら（水族館）はトミーのような障がいのある子も歓迎して，ロージーに会わせてくれるのです。

D **Summary Practice:** Fill in the blanks with suitable words beginning with the letters indicated. Then listen to the CD and check your answers.

DL 10 CD1-16

OdySea (1. **A**) in the state of (2. **A**) is the home of Rosie the Penguin, a superstar among children with (3. **s**) (4. **n**). Like many of them, Rosie has faced serious physical (5. **c**). Although she was (6. **h**), the zookeepers realized that Rosie was unable to sit up because her (7. **f**) were (8. **m**). They came up with a clever way to (9. **s**) her leg (10. **m**), using a baby onesie and (11. **s**) made of (12. **e**). With the help of the (13. **a**) (14. **c**) (15. **t**), Rosie was eventually able to sit up, then take small (16. **s**) and finally, to (17. **w**) on her own. (18. **C**) facing their own challenges are inspired by Rosie's unique (19. **s**), with some visitors even sending messages of (20. **t**). Go, Rosie!

E **Discussion:** Share your ideas and opinions with your classmates.

1. Penguins are among the most popular animals in zoos and aquariums. Do an internet search to learn more about them. Share your findings with your classmates.

2. Look for stories about other creative programs to inspire people with special needs.

Pronunciation Hints from the News 1

外来語や地名の発音

日本語のカタカナ発音と英語の発音が異なる場合，特に外来語や地名などでは，アクセントの位置を含めて注意が必要である。本ニュースストーリーに登場するpenguinは「ペンギン」にならないよう，/g/の音を入れて「ペングイン」と発音するとよい。

ペンギン	penguin	[péŋgwɪn]
ウクライナ	Ukraine	[ju:kréin]
ガラパゴス	Galapagos	[gəlá:pəgous]
エクアドル	Ecuador	[ékwədɔ̀:ɚ]
ロシア	Russia	[rʌ́ʃə]
アウシュビッツ	Auschwitz	[áʊʃvɪts]

—They want you to meet Rosie the ***Penguin***… *(Penguin at Arizona Aquarium, P.21 L.2)*

—…, both young and old standing in solidarity with prayers and protests for peace in ***Ukraine***. *(Standing in Solidarity, P.41 L.1)*

—…, some proudly waving the blue and yellow flag of ***Ukraine.*** *(Standing in Solidarity, P.42 L.21)*

—Ninety-six percent of the ***Galapagos*** Islands are protected by ***Ecuador***'s ***Galapagos*** Marine Reserve… *(Saving the Galapagos, P.68 L.22)*

—Factors driving the price spikes include everything from ***Russia***'s invasion of ***Ukraine*** to supply chain snafus. *(Rising Prices, P.81 L.23)*

—The children of ***Auschwitz***, the survivors, going back. *(International Holocaust Remembrance Day, P.86 L.3)*

News Story

4

Air Date: April 18, 2022
Duration: 1'50"

Colorado River Most Endangered

The Gist

- What is the current situation of the Colorado River?
- What are some of the negative effects?

Before You Watch the News *Warm-up Exercises*

A Vocabulary Check: Choose the correct definition for each of the words below.

DL 11 CD1-17

1. ominous	( )	a.	to gradually decrease in amount
2. unprecedented	( )	b.	to drop or fall at high speed
3. reserves	( )	c.	threatening; menacing
4. plummet	( )	d.	stock for future use
5. dwindle	( )	e.	something that has never happened before

B Fill in the blanks with appropriate expressions from the Vocabulary Check above. Change the word forms where necessary.

1. The campers feared their ( ) food supply might not last until they were found.
2. Check out those ( ) clouds. The storm's heading this way.
3. The climber lost his balance and ( ) to the ground.
4. An ( ) number of retirees are deciding to continue their education.
5. That region has significant coal ( ) that might be needed someday.

Focus on the News Story

D. Muir: This week, we are reporting here, on the leadup to Earth Day. And tonight, the alarming new report on the Colorado River. Forty million Americans depend on the water from that river. We have reported here on this broadcast on the conditions in that river before. Tonight, our team is back amid these troubling new findings. Here's ABC's Kayna Whitworth now.

K. Whitworth: Tonight, an ominous new report from a conservation group, naming the Colorado River 1. ______________________________ .

M. Rice, American Rivers: We're facing an unprecedented crisis.

K. Whitworth: Forty million people depend on the river daily. And since 2000, water levels have dropped 20 percent, threatening the environment, agriculture, and reliable water supplies as it winds through seven states. Major cities throughout the Southwest rely on the Colorado River.

B. Udall, Sr. Water & Climate Research Scientist, Colorado State Univ.: ...all saying the LA Basin, maybe a quarter of their water supply comes out of the Colorado River. Las Vegas is 2. ______________________________ .

K. Whitworth: Reserves in Lake Powell and Lake Mead plummeting to all-time lows.

P. Brouche, Rancher: We haven't irrigated our lawn in four years.

K. Whitworth: Fifth-generation Colorado ranchers Paul and Doug Brouche trying to conserve the dwindling water by building cobblestone riffles, [3.] ____.

As part of one of the largest restoration efforts on the Upper Basin, you have installed five of these riffles right there along a 12-mile stretch?

P. Brouche: That is correct. It is this region's adaptation to climate change.

K. Whitworth: Experts say as the landscape continues to dry, water levels could drop another 10 to 20 percent by 2050.

M. Rice: So, we're faced with this, this new reality where [4.] ____.

K. Whitworth: David, $8.3 billion from the infrastructure bill has been earmarked for western water. And all along the Colorado River, they have hundreds of vetted, shovel-ready projects, but it takes a collective effort [5.] ________________________________, and everyone I spoke with said time is running out. David?

Notes
L.1 **Earth Day** 「アースデー；地球の日〈地球環境についての意識を高めるための日。毎年4月22日〉」
L.2 **Colorado River** 「コロラド川〈ロッキー山脈からアリゾナ州の南部へと流れる〉」
L.10 **American Rivers** 「アメリカン・リバーズ〈河川生態系の保護などを目的に 1973 年に設立された環境 NPO 団体〉」
L.14 **the Southwest** 「アメリカの南西部」
L.16 **Sr. Water & Climate Research Scientist** 「水資源・気候に関する主任研究科学者」
L.17 **LA Basin** 「ロサンゼルス盆地」
L.20 **Lake Powell** 「パウエル湖〈コロラド川の途中にある貯水池［人工湖］で，ユタ州とアリゾナ州にまたがる〉」
L.20 **Lake Mead** 「ミード湖〈コロラド川をせき止めたフーバー・ダムによって作られたアメリカ最大の貯水量を誇る貯水池〉」
L.24 **cobblestone riffles** 「石畳による浅瀬〈川の一部に石を並べて水の流れを制限することで，浅瀬を作り出している〉」
L.27 **Upper Basin** 「アッパー・ベイシン；(コロラド川) 上流域〈= the Upper Colorado River Basin コロラド，ニューメキシコ，ユタ，ワイオミングの4州にまたがるコロラド川の上流域〉」
L.35 **infrastructure bill** 「インフラ投資法〈2021 年 11 月，バイデン大統領は国内のインフラ強化を目的とした1兆ドル（約 110 兆円）規模のインフラ法案に署名し，同法が成立した〉」
L.37 **vetted, shovel-ready projects** 「審査済みのすぐに着工できる（建設などの）プロジェクト（事業）」

After You Watch the News *Exercises*

A Listen to the news story and fill in the blanks in the text.

B **Multiple Choice Questions:** Select the best answer to each question.

1. Which of the following statements is true regarding the Colorado River?
   a. Its reserves have been gone for four years.
   b. The water levels have dropped 20 percent in one year.
   c. It serves millions of people spread over seven states.

2. What is affected by the drastic drop in water levels of the river?
   a. reserves in area lakes and irrigation practices
   b. the water supply throughout much of the Southwest
   c. both ***a*** and ***b***

3. The cobblestone riffles created by Paul and Doug Brouche
   a. are part of an $8.3 billion restoration effort.
   b. are an attempt to keep the water level high.
   c. have been placed all along the Colorado River.

4. The Colorado River
   a. may continue to face a severe drop in water levels.
   b. will soon improve using money from the infrastructure bill.
   c. is likely to improve as the river adapts naturally to climate change.

C Translate the following Japanese into English. Then listen to the CD and practice the conversation with your partner. DL 12 CD1-20

A: Hey, Doug! How's your project coming along?
B: It's a lot of work, but we're doing it to make the river healthier.
A: 1. They say ______________________________.
B: I think it is! But there's a lot more to do.
A: 2. ______________________________
______________________________?
B: 3. ______________________________,
but it's just not easy to put that money to use.
A: This is an unprecedented crisis. I hope something happens soon.

1. 現在行われている最大級の修復作業だそうですね。
2. 西部の水資源に充当されたインフラ法案の数十億ドルはどうなりましたか。
3. すぐにでも実行できる何百もの審査済みのプロジェクトがありますが，そのお金を活用するのは簡単なことではありません。

D Summary Practice: Fill in the blanks with suitable words beginning with the letters indicated. Then listen to the CD and check your answers.

DL 13 CD1-21

An alarming new report from a (1. **c**) group has identified the (2. **C**) River as being the most (3. **e**) river in the entire country. For the (4. **f**) (5. **m**) Americans who depend on that river every day, it is an (6. **o**) reminder of the effects of (7. **c**) (8. **c**). With water (9. **l**) dropping (10. **t**) percent since 2000, residents of cities as far away as (11. **L**) (12. **V**) are feeling the pinch. To compound the problem, the (13. **r**) in some nearby lakes have (14. **p**) to their lowest levels ever. Faced with having to live with less (15. **w**), Paul and Doug Brouche have snapped into action, constructing five (16. **c**) (17. **r**) to help (18. **c**) the (19. **d**) water supply. Let's hope it's not too late.

E Discussion: Share your ideas and opinions with your classmates.

1. What is the condition of rivers in Japan? Are there any major rivers in your city or prefecture? Are there any rivers considered to be endangered? If so, what efforts are being made to improve their condition?

2. According to the news story, the drop in water level of the Colorado River is due to climate change. What are other effects of global warming? Have there been any negative effects in the region where you live?

3. Look at the U.S. map in the back of your textbook (pp. 108–109). Can you identify other states and cities in the Southwest? Select one of the states, cities, lakes or geographic areas mentioned in this news story and look online to find more information about it. Share it with your classmates.

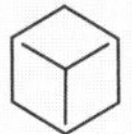

Useful Grammar from the News

間接話法

ニュース英語では，引用符（“ ”）を用いて発言者の言葉をそのまま伝える直接話法はほとんど用いられず，伝え手が発言者の話した内容を自分の言葉に言い換えて伝える間接話法が頻繁に使われる。その際，A said to B that ~「AはBに対して~と言った」という「B（聞き手）」にあたる目的語と接続詞のthatは省略されることが多い。間接話法の場合，通常はさまざまな種類の伝達動詞（ask, order, answer, contend, mention, maintainなど）が用いられるが，ニュース英語では平叙文がほとんどであるため，伝達動詞は話しことばでよく用いられるsayが多用される。

—Experts ***say*** as the landscape continues to dry, water levels could drop another 10 to 20 percent by 2050. (*Colorado River Most Endangered, P.29 L.31*)

—Scientists ***say*** the ship's condition has been preserved all these years... (*Endurance Ship Found in Antarctica, P.47 L.10*)

—I sat down with Francine and David Wheeler, who ***said*** they joined the lawsuit... (*Historic Gunmaker Settlement, P.61 L.30*)

—And, David, the families ***saying*** today, this is not about the money. (*Historic Gunmaker Settlement, P.62 L.43*)

—Their population, scientists ***say***, are now becoming a barometer of climate change. (*Saving the Galapagos, P.67 L.14*)

—And they ***say*** it's directly attributed to inflation. (*Rising Prices, P.81 L.36*)

—She told us why that day, ***saying*** it's important that... (*International Holocaust Remembrance Day, P.87 L.31*)

—She ***said*** it took 232 years, 115 appointments for a black woman... (*Historic Confirmation, P.100 L.5*)

—...Biden ***said*** when he decided to run, he envisioned this very moment, ... (*Historic Confirmation, P.102 L.55*)

Controversial "Don't Say Gay" Bill

The Gist
- What new law is expected to be passed in Florida?
- What do critics of the legislation say?

Before You Watch the News — *Warm-up Exercises*

A Vocabulary Check: Choose the correct definition for each of the words below.

DL 14 CD1-22

1. controversial ( ) a. to nickname; to unofficially label
2. dub ( ) b. to exclude from a group
3. engage in ( ) c. to express strong disapproval of
4. ostracize ( ) d. disputed; giving rise to public disagreement
5. condemn ( ) e. to be involved in

B Fill in the blanks with appropriate expressions from the Vocabulary Check above. Change the word forms where necessary.

1. The PTA is encouraging parents to get more ( ) school activities.
2. Joe was ( ) King of the Track when he won the marathon for the third year in a row.
3. You shouldn't ( ) Chris until you know all the facts. He may be innocent.
4. If you feel ( ), you should see a counselor. It's better to get help.
5. The school board insisted that the ( ) poster be taken down immediately.

Focus on the News Story

D. Muir: Meantime back here at home tonight, and to Florida's controversial legislation passing. Now sent to the governor there, tonight. It's called the Parental Rights in Education Bill. Critics call it the "Don't Say Gay" bill. What it would prevent teachers from saying or doing, and some asking tonight, 1. ______________________________, what about isolated or bullied children? Who will they be able to turn to at school? Here's Victor Oquendo, in Florida, tonight.

V. Oquendo: Tonight, Florida's controversial legislation, dubbed by critics as the "Don't Say Gay" bill and gaining national attention, has been sent to Governor Ron DeSantis to sign, the governor already signaling he supports it. The State Senate passing the bill 22-17, today, 2. ____ from the LGBTQ community and thousands of students.

Officially called the Parental Rights in Education Bill, the measure bans lessons regarding sexual orientation or gender identity in grades K through third, and any instruction "that is not age appropriate or developmentally appropriate," 3. ___________________ __________________________________. Those standards, however, not yet in place for several grades.

J. Harding, Florida State Representative: All it does is state what is age... talks about ah... what's appropriate in the classroom to teach. And then it talks about the fact that the parent has the right to be engaged in the education of their children.

Protesters: We say gay! We say gay!

V. Oquendo: But critics warn 4. ____ from helping children who feel bullied or ostracized and have nowhere to turn.

According to The Trevor Project, 52 percent of LGBTQ youth enrolled in middle or high school reported being bullied in the last year, and 42 percent reported seriously considering suicide.

President Biden has already condemned the bill. And tonight, 5. ____ schools implementing it could lose access to federal grants due to a 1972 law. David?

Notes

L.3 **Parental Rights in Education Bill** 「教育における親の権利法案」

L.3 **“Don't Say Gay” bill** 「『ゲイと言ってはいけない』法案」

L.10 **Governor Ron DeSantis** 「ロン・デサンティス（フロリダ州）知事」

L.13 **LGBTQ** 「エル・ジー・ビー・ティー・キュー：性的少数者（マイノリティー）〈lesbian, gay, bisexual, transgender and queer の略。Q は questioning を表すこともあり，自分の性的指向を明確に決めていない人を指す〉」

L.16 **grades K through third** 「グレード K からグレード 3〈幼稚園年長から小学 3 年生までの生徒。アメリカの義務教育は，日本の幼稚園年長にあたる歳から始まる。このグレードを K（kindergarten）と呼び，グレード K～12 が一般的な義務教育期間で，「K-12」と略称される〉」

L.20 **All it does is state ... in the classroom to teach.** 「それ［法案］は，教室で教えるのに年齢的に適切なものは何かということを述べているだけなのです。〈“All it does is what is age appropriate in the classroom to teach.” と言いたかったものと思われる〉」

L.28 **The Trevor Project** 「トレバー・プロジェクト〈1998 年に設立された米国の非営利団体で，LGBTQ の若者の自殺防止活動に注力する全米屈指の組織〉」

L.33 **federal grants** 「連邦補助金」

L.34 **1972 law** 「1972 年の法律〈＝教育改正法第 9 編 連邦政府からの補助金を受けている教育機関において，性別による差別を禁止した連邦法〉」

Background of the News

共和党のデサンティス(DeSantis)知事が2022年３月28日に署名し，成立したフロリダ州の新法，通称「ゲイと言ってはいけない」法(“Don't Say Gay” bill)が物議を醸している。同法は，主に小学校で性的指向(sexual orientation)や性自認(gender identity)について話題にすることを禁止するもので，学校が子どもに提供するメンタルヘルス面などのケアも親が拒否できるなど，子どもの教育における親の権利強化をうたっている。民主党は，性的少数者(LGBTQ)の子どもへのいじめ(bullying)や差別につながるとしてこれに強く反対し，バイデン大統領も非難している。2022年４月７日付の『日経速報ニュースアーカイブ』によると，この法案(legislation)をめぐっては，同州のウォルト・ディズニーなどといった民間企業からも，性の多様性を損なうとして反対の声があがっていたが，2022年７月１日，同州法は施行された。

南部テキサス州やルイジアナ州，中西部オクラホマ州など，共和党優勢の他の州でもフロリダ州と同様の法律が制定されている。フロリダ州は他州の州法よりも一歩踏みこんだ内容となっており，法律に違反していると親が判断した場合，親はその学区を訴え，損害賠償を求めることも可能としている。

After You Watch the News — *Exercises*

A Listen to the news story and fill in the blanks in the text.

B **Multiple Choice Questions:** Select the best answer to each question.

1. The Parental Rights in Education Bill
   a. has the support of President Biden.
   b. has just been signed into law in Florida.
   c. passed the State Senate despite protests.

2. “Don't Say Gay”
   a. refers to a newly proposed law supporting gay students.
   b. is the nickname used by people critical of the new Florida legislation.
   c. is Governor DeSantis' nickname for the Parental Rights in Education Bill.

3. Which statement is ***NOT*** true regarding the proposed bill?
   a. It has many critics among the LGBTQ community.
   b. It aims to ban lessons on gender identity in the early grades.
   c. State standards are fully in place for all grades.

4. Critics of the Florida bill
   a. include 52 percent of LGBTQ youth.
   b. are asking parents to be more engaged.
   c. are concerned that gay youth will have less support.

C Translate the following Japanese into English. Then listen to the CD and practice the conversation with your partner. DL 15 CD1-25

A: Hey, look at that group of protesters. What do those signs say?
B: "Don't Say Gay!"
A: 1. Oh, ______________________________
______________.
B: Aren't they too late?
A: 2. ______________________________
______________________.
B: 3. ______________________________?
Even the president has condemned it.
A: That's a good question. We'll have to see what happens.

1. ああ，彼らは新しい教育における親の権利法案に抗議しているのでしょう。
2. フロリダ州上院で可決されましたが，デサンティス知事がまだ署名していません。
3. こんなに物議を醸しているのに，どうして法律になってしまうのでしょう。

D **Summary Practice:** Fill in the blanks with suitable words beginning with the letters indicated. Then listen to the CD and check your answers.

DL 16 CD1-26

The Trevor (1. **P**) has released some alarming statistics regarding LGBTQ (2. **y**). The group claims that fully 52 percent of gay students in (3. **m**) and (4. **h**) school have reported being (5. **b**), and 42 percent have thought seriously about (6. **s**). This has many people (7. **c**) Florida's (8. **c**) Parental Rights in (9. **E**) Bill. (10. **D**) the "Don't Say Gay" bill by its many critics, the proposed legislature passed the State (11. **S**) 22 to 17 and is now waiting to be signed by the (12. **g**), who seems inclined to support it. Among other things, the proposed law aims to (13. **b**) lessons on sexual (14. **o**) and gender (15. **i**) in the early grades. Defenders of the bill, like (16. **S**) (17. **R**) Harding, insist that the bill simply focuses on what's (18. **a**) to teach in the classroom and on the right of (19. **p**) to be involved in their children's education. Amid chants of "We say (20. **g**)," the controversy is not over yet.

E **Discussion:** Share your ideas and opinions with your classmates.

1. Do an internet search for updates on Florida's Parental Rights in Education Bill. See if you can find other recent legislation targeting the LGBTQ community.
2. What is the current situation of the LGBTQ community in Japan? Has it changed at all in recent years? Is gay marriage legal?
3. How do you feel about the new legislation in the state of Florida? Discuss some potential positive and negative effects. Can you imagine such a law being passed here in Japan? Discuss your answers in a group.

Standing in Solidarity

The Gist
- What is the situation in Ukraine?
- How are Ukrainian Americans showing their support?

Before You Watch the News *Warm-up Exercises*

A Vocabulary Check: Choose the correct definition for each of the words below.

DL 17 CD1-27

1. solidarity ( ) a. to comfort
2. seek ( ) b. to search for; to attempt to find
3. hymn ( ) c. to reunite; to gather together
4. soothe ( ) d. unity; a strong feeling of support
5. rally (v.) ( ) e. a religious song, usually sung in church

B Fill in the blanks with appropriate expressions from the Vocabulary Check above. Change the word forms where necessary.

1. We enjoyed hearing the ( ) sung by the choir in the cathedral in France.
2. The brave troops ( ) and finally defeated the enemy.
3. The sick child was ( ) by her mother's bedtime song.
4. Their homes destroyed by the hurricane, hundreds of people were left ( ) shelter.
5. The new mayor vowed to work on building ( ) in the community.

Focus on the News Story

L. Davis: Finally, tonight, here in the U.S., both young and old standing in solidarity with prayers and protests for peace in Ukraine.

From protests to prayer, across the country, Ukrainian Americans are coming together, seeking peace. Familiar hymns soothing these parishioners at the Guardian Angel Roman Catholic Church in Brooklyn, 1. ____ ____________________.

Supporter 1: It's heartbreaking, especially when like fathers leave home and leave their children. And they know that they are going to stay because they need to fight.

L. Davis: This woman, originally from Ukraine, 2. ______________________ ____ in Pittsfield, Massachusetts.

Supporter 2: I want to say to our European allies...

L. Davis: Others united this weekend to rally in support of their home country. From Portland, Oregon...

Supporter 3: These are people that love their country and 3. ____________ ______________________________.

Supporter 4: Harvard stands with Ukraine.

L. Davis: ...to Cambridge, Massachusetts, where more than 500 students gathered at a rally in Harvard Yard, some proudly waving the blue and yellow flag of Ukraine.

Supporter 5: Many of my classmates, as well as friends, 4. ____________________ ______________________________ and, perhaps, they might die.

L. Davis: And in Los Angeles...

Supporter 6: I have family in Ukraine. For the last two days, they've been careful. They've been hiding. 5. ______________________________ __________. They're packed to go, but they're staying their ground.

L. Davis: ...solidarity in the streets, a world away.

Supporter 7: Ukraine, stay strong. Stop the war!

L. Davis: 6. ____ ________________. Thanks so much for watching. David Muir, right back here tomorrow night. I'm Linsey Davis in New York. Have a great evening. Good night.

Notes L.5 **parishioners** 「(教会の) 教区民」

L.5 **the Guardian Angel Roman Catholic Church** 「ガーディアン・エンジェル・ローマ・カトリック教会〈ニューヨーク市のブルックリンにある1880年創立の教会〉」

L.6 **Brooklyn** 「ブルックリン〈ニューヨーク市南部の区で，ロングアイランド西部に位置する〉」

L.12 **Pittsfield** 「ピッツフィールド〈マサチューセッツ州西部の都市〉」

L.16 **Portland** 「ポートランド〈オレゴン州の北西部に位置する同州最大の都市〉」

L.20 **Cambridge** 「ケンブリッジ〈マサチューセッツ州のハーバード大学，マサチューセッツ工科大学のある都市〉」

L.21 **Harvard Yard** 「ハーバード・ヤード〈ハーバード大学のキャンパスの中で最も古い地区で，新入生寮，図書館，メモリアル教会などがある〉」

L.28 **staying their ground** 「(じっと我慢して) 動かない；自分の立場を貫こうとしている」

L.29 **a world away** 「遠く離れた地で」

After You Watch the News — *Exercises*

A Listen to the news story and fill in the blanks in the text.

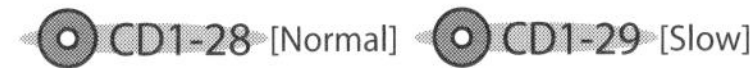

B **Multiple Choice Questions:** Select the best answer to each question.

1. What are Americans doing to show their support of people in Ukraine?
   a. praying and protesting
   b. turning out all of the lights
   c. selling blue and yellow flags at rallies

2. Some of the Ukrainian Americans in the newscast
   a. are trying to return to their home country.
   b. are hiding from family members in Ukraine.
   c. worry about friends and relatives who could die in the war.

3. Among the Ukraine supporters featured in the news story are
   a. many European allies.
   b. people from all across the United States.
   c. people who will go to Ukraine to fight.

4. What are the supporters concerned about?
   a. fathers who leave their children to go to war
   b. people who are prepared to leave but are staying put
   c. both ***a*** and ***b***

C Translate the following Japanese into English. Then listen to the CD and practice the conversation with your partner.

DL 18 CD1-30

A: Look at that crowd! Where are they all going?

B: To Harvard Yard. 1. ______________________________.

A: What are they carrying?

B: 2. ______________________________.
They'll be waving them to show their solidarity.

A: Let's join them!

B: Good idea. The Ukrainians need our support. 3. ______________________________
______________________________.

A: Hey, I have some cloth upstairs. Let's make some flags.

1. 今夜ウクライナを支援するための集会があります。
2. あれらはウクライナの青と黄の旗です。
3. 彼らは自国を愛し，ただ自由になりたいと思っているだけなのです。

D **Summary Practice:** Fill in the blanks with suitable words beginning with the letters indicated. Then listen to the CD and check your answers.

DL 19 CD1-31

All across the U.S., people are turning out to show their (1. **s**) with (2. **U**). (3. **P**) for (4. **p**) at the Guardian Angel Roman (5. **C**) (6. **C**), Ukrainian Americans are comforted by singing soothing (7. **h**). Elsewhere, more than (8. **f**) (9. **h**) students gathered at a (10. **r**) at Harvard University, proudly (11. **w**) Ukrainian (12. **f**). Many of the (13. **s**) have family in Ukraine and others are (14. **o**) from Ukraine themselves. All are concerned about the (15. **f**) leaving their (16. **c**) to go fight, and realize that their loved ones who fight in the (17. **w**) could (18. **d**). The war may be a world away, but the prayers and (19. **p**) will give the Ukrainians who (20. **l**) their country some hope.

E Discussion: Share your ideas and opinions with your classmates.

1. How much do you know about Ukraine? Do an internet search about some aspect of the country or culture that interests you. Share your findings with the class.
2. At the time this news story was originally broadcast, the war in Ukraine had just started. What has happened since then? Find information about the number of Ukrainians who lost their lives or were displaced as a result of the war.
3. How did people here in Japan support the Ukrainian people during and after the Russian invasion? How many Ukrainians sought refuge in this country? What kinds of support did they receive from the Japanese government and other sources?

News Story

7

Air Date: March 9, 2022
Duration: 1'51"

Endurance Ship Found in Antarctica

The Gist
- What happened to the Endurance in 1915?
- Why is the recent discovery so amazing?

Before You Watch the News *Warm-up Exercises*

A Vocabulary Check: Choose the correct definition for each of the words below.

DL 20 CD1-32

1. remarkable	( )	**a.**	harsh; severe
2. intact	( )	**b.**	whole; undamaged
3. preserve	( )	**c.**	to give one's opinion
4. brutal	( )	**d.**	extraordinary; amazing
5. weigh in	( )	**e.**	to conserve; to maintain

B Fill in the blanks with appropriate expressions from the Vocabulary Check above. Change the word forms where necessary.

1. A dried flower from Grandma's wedding bouquet is carefully ( ) in the family Bible.
2. Ken has made ( ) progress in Italian in just eight months.
3. We need everyone on the staff to ( ) before making a final decision.
4. The typhoon winds were ( )! Several of our trees lost branches.
5. We were surprised to find that the package was still ( ) after the long, bumpy ride.

Focus on the News Story

D. Muir: Finally tonight here, the famous ship lost more than a century ago, finally found.

Tonight, the remarkable discovery, nearly 10,000 feet below the surface at the bottom of Antarctica's Weddell Sea. The Endurance, one of history's greatest shipwrecks, now finally found. This is the first time it's been seen [1.] ______________________________ __________. The bow, the ship's wheel and rear deck, the stern, with the name Endurance still intact in gold letters. National Geographic, part of our parent company, Disney, giving ABC News this exclusive first look at one of the masts. Scientists say the ship's condition has been preserved all these years [2.] ______________ ______________________________ and the lack of microorganisms.

The Endurance sank in 1915. Sir Ernest Shackleton and a crew of 27 were attempting to be the first to cross Antarctica when they got trapped by the ice. After months, the ice eventually crushed and then sank the ship. These images were brought back and played in theaters. [3.] ______________________________ and lived on ice drifts for months through the brutal polar winter, before making their way eventually to safety. Now, after more than a century, the expedition called Endurance 22 making the discovery.

Expert: From the stern, and off to the starboard side, slightly.

D. Muir: Deepwater submersibles using sonar to comb the seafloor for hours. And right here, tonight...

D. Snow, historian: Hi, David.

D. Muir: ...historian Dan Snow with the expedition team, [4.] ______________________________ studying sea ice as the world warms. Tonight, he weighs in on their discovery.

D. Snow: I think this matters, because it will inspire generations [5.] ______________________________.

D. Muir: It's inspired us. Remarkable to see it so well preserved under the sea. I'll see you tomorrow. Good night.

Notes

L.4 **Weddell Sea** 「ウェッデル海〈南極半島の東方に位置し，南極海の一部を構成する海域〉」

L.4 **The Endurance** 「エンデュアランス号」

L.8 **National Geographic** 「ナショナル・ジオグラフィック〈正式にはナショナル・ジオグラフィック・パートナーズ（National Geographic Partners）。ウォルト・ディズニー社とナショナル・ジオグラフィック協会との合弁会社。また，ウォルト・ディズニー社は 1995 年，米三大ネットワークの一つである ABC 放送を買収した〉」

L.13 **microorganisms** 「微生物」

L.14 **Sir Ernest Shackleton** 「アーネスト・シャクルトン卿〈英国の探検家（1874 ～ 1922 年）。南極大陸横断を目指して 1914 年にエンデュアランス号（The Endurance）に乗って出発し，流氷の海で座礁したが，27 名の隊員と共に奇跡の生還を果たした〉」

L.22 **starboard** 「右舷」

Background of the News

1915年に南極大陸(Antarctica)沖で沈没した探検船「エンデュアランス号」(The Endurance)を海底で発見したと，海洋史跡の保護に取り組む「フォークランド海洋遺産財団」の調査チームが発表した。2022年4月4日付の『読売新聞』によると，木造の船がほとんど当時の状態のまま残っており，「画期的な発見だ」(remarkable discovery)としている。アーネスト・シャクルトン(Sir Ernest Shackleton)率いる英国隊は，当時まだ行われていなかった南極大陸徒歩横断に挑戦するため，1914年12月に300トンの木造帆船エンデュアランス号でロンドンを出航した。しかし，シャクルトンと27人の乗組員(crew)を乗せた船はウェッデル海(Weddell Sea)の流氷に閉じ込められ，一行の消息は途絶する。船をあきらめた探検隊は，海氷上に張ったテントや無人島で過ごし，1年以上に及ぶ漂流にもかかわらず，全隊員が生還を果たした。

シャクルトンの探検の軌跡は，2000年に，『エンデュアランス号大漂流』(E・C・キメル著)として出版され，本ニュースストーリーでも紹介されているように，持ち帰られた映像を元に映画も公開された。

After You Watch the News — *Exercises*

A Listen to the news story and fill in the blanks in the text.

B **Multiple Choice Questions:** Select the best answer to each question.

1. Which statement describes the condition of the Endurance when it was finally found?
   - a. It was mostly intact, but the mast was crushed by the ice.
   - b. It was well preserved due to the cold temperature of the Weddell Sea.
   - c. Most of the bow and stern were intact, but the ship's name was worn off.

2. The crew of the Endurance
   - a. played an important role in the discovery of the ship.
   - b. lost their lives in the icy water following the shipwreck.
   - c. managed to survive through the winter and make their way to safety.

3. Which statement is ***NOT*** true about the discovery of the Endurance?
   a. It is the subject of a popular new movie called "Endurance 22."
   b. It took place more than a century after it sank.
   c. It involves what is called one of history's greatest shipwrecks.

4. Sir Ernest Shackleton's crew
   a. included ice researchers studying sea ice.
   b. was part of an expedition named Endurance 22.
   c. was attempting to cross Antarctica when it was shipwrecked.

C Translate the following Japanese into English. Then listen to the CD and practice the conversation with your partner. DL 21 CD1-35

A: Did you hear the Endurance has finally been found?
B: No way! That's the ship that sank in Antarctica back in 1915, right?
A: That's it. 1. ______________________________
______________.
B: And they actually found it! Incredible!
A: 2. ______________________________.
B: It must be in terrible condition if it's been under water for such a long time.
A: 3. That's what they expected, but ______________________________
____
______________.

1. 深海潜水艇がソナーを使って何時間も海底を調べました。
2. エンデュアランス号は１世紀以上も行方不明だったのです。
3. それが彼らの予想でしたが，科学者たちは，氷のような温度と微生物がいないことを理由に，船の状態が保たれたと言います。

D Summary Practice: Fill in the blanks with suitable words beginning with the letters indicated. Then listen to the CD and check your answers.

DL 22 CD1-36

Over a (1. **c**) ago, Sir Ernest (2. **S**) and his (3. **c**) of 27 attempted to be the first ever to cross (4. **A**) in their ship, the (5. **E**). In one of the most famous (6. **s**) in history, the Endurance sunk to the bottom of the (7. **W**) (8. **S**) where it remained for 107 years. Amazingly, due to the (9. **i**) (10. **t**) of the sea and the lack of (11. **m**), the ship's (12. **c**) was (13. **p**) during the long passage of time. The story of the ship's crew, who lived on ice (14. **d**) throughout the (15. **b**) winter and eventually made their way to (16. **s**), stirs the imagination. Historian Dan Snow, who joined the (17. **e**) team along with several (18. **i**) researchers, believes that the discovery is sure to inspire (19. **g**) with a love of (20. **e**) and adventure.

E Discussion: Share your ideas and opinions with your classmates.

1. Do an internet search to learn more about the Endurance and its crew's incredible story of survival.
2. The National Geographic Society is involved in exploring and teaching about our amazing world. Their stories are available through the National Geographic Channel, National Geographic Magazine, and on YouTube. Check out a topic that interests you and share it with your classmates.
3. Shipwrecks are often featured in books and movies enjoyed by children and adults alike. Do you have any favorite stories or movies that involve a shipwreck?

News Story

8

Air Date: February 2, 2022
Duration: 1'59"

An Inspiring Child Author

The Gist
- Why is an eight-year-old in the news tonight?
- What was the reaction to what he did?

Before You Watch the News — *Warm-up Exercises*

A Vocabulary Check: Choose the correct definition for each of the words below.

DL 23 CD2-02

1. aspiring ( ) a. to have a strong wish or desire
2. long (v.) ( ) b. to roughly calculate
3. a hit ( ) c. giving someone a positive or creative feeling
4. inspiring ( ) d. a great success
5. estimate (v.) ( ) e. directing one's hopes towards becoming something

B Fill in the blanks with appropriate expressions from the Vocabulary Check above. Change the word forms where necessary.

1. We were required to ( ) the total cost of the damage done by the flood.
2. Meg is a talented musician and her sister is an ( ) veterinarian.
3. Although Tim ( ) to get a dog, it was against regulations to have pets in his apartment building.
4. That group had many ( ) several years back, but we haven't heard anything from them for a long time.
5. Mr. Jeffries was the most ( ) teacher I've ever known.

Focus on the News Story

D. Muir: Finally tonight here, "America Strong." The eight-year-old author and his new book. If you'd like to read it, there's a long line. A two-year wait.

Tonight, in Boise, Idaho, at the Lake Hazel Branch of the Ada Community Library, 1. ____________________ is an eight-year-old boy, "America Strong." Dillon Helbig took an old journal his grandmother gave him and turned it into an 82-page book, writing the title right there, *The Adventures of Dillon Helbig's Crismis by Dillon Helbig, hisself.* 2. ____________________. Dillon is the main character. Chapter One, "To the North Pole." And like many aspiring authors, Dillon longed to see his book on the library shelf. So, he made it happen himself, sneaking his book onto the shelf. The librarians found it and 3. ____________________. It was a hit. And the next time Dillon came back to the library, they asked if they could make it an official library book. Right here, tonight...

D. Helbig, author of The Adventures of Dillon Helbig's Crismis*:* Hi, David.

D. Muir: The new author and his book...

D. Helbig: One day...

D. Muir: ...reading it to us.

D. Helbig: ...I was decorating the tree, and the tree fell.

D. Muir: Dillon telling us why he wanted other children to read his book.

D. Helbig: When one person sees me do this, [4] ______________________________ __________. And that is inspiring.

D. Muir: There is now a 64-person wait list for Dillon's book. The library estimates that'll take about two years for everyone to sign it out.

S. Helbig, mother of Dillon: Hi, David.

A. Helbig, father of Dillon: Hey, David.

D. Muir: Dillon's parents, Susan and Alex.

S. Helbig: The inspiration for other children and adults alike, I think, is..., um, ... the best part of this all.

A. Helbig: If you believe in yourself, and you can make your dream happen, and that's what he did.

D. Muir: And, tonight, [5] ____ ________________________________.

D. Helbig: Thanks for your time, David. Bye.

D. Muir: Thank you. Dillon Helbig, remember that name. He's just getting started. Go, Dillon and I'll see you right back here, tomorrow night. Good night.

Notes

- L.4 **Boise** 「ボイシ［ボイジ］〈アイダホ州の州都〉」
- L.4 **Lake Hazel Branch of the Ada Community Library** 「エイダ地区図書館のレイクヘイゼル分館〈アイダホ州の公立図書館〉」
- L.9 ***The Adventures of Dillon Helbig's Crismis by Dillion Helbig, hisself*** 「『ディロン・ヘルビッグのクリスミス［クリスマス］の冒険，ディロン・ヘルビッグ本人による』〈スペルの間違いはそのままになっている〉」
- L.9 ***hisself*** 「= himself〈本の表紙に書かれたタイトルを忠実に発音している〉」
- L.26 **The library estimates that'll take about two years...** 「= The library estimates that *it'll* take about two years...〈文法的には that'll は that it'll になる〉」

After You Watch the News　*Exercises*

A Listen to the news story and fill in the blanks in the text.

B **Multiple Choice Questions:** Select the best answer to each question.

1. Dillon Helbig's book

a. took two years to write.

b. is a story about the author himself.

c. was inspired by a book from the library.

2. Which statement is ***NOT*** true about the Lake Hazel Branch of the Ada Community Library?

a. Dillon hid his book on a shelf there.

b. The library paid Dillon for his book.

c. The employees made Dillon's book an official library book.

3. *The Adventures of Dillon Helbig's Crismis*

a. was written by Dillon with help from his grandmother.

b. is based on a story that Dillon's grandmother told him.

c. was written in a journal that Dillon's grandmother gave him.

4. What does Dillon ***NOT*** plan to do in the future?

   a. become a librarian

   b. write more books

   c. inspire other people to write books

C Translate the following Japanese into English. Then listen to the CD and practice the conversation with your partner.

DL 24 CD2-05

A: I just got a call from the library. I can pick up the book tomorrow.

B: What book?

A: Dillon's Christmas book! 1. ____
________________________.

B: How long have you been waiting?

A: 2. ____.

B: 3. Gee, ____.

A: Really! We should encourage our own kids to write. You never know what might happen!

1. 今，図書館で一番人気の本なのです。
2. １年以上前から順番待ちです。
3. うわ～，８歳の子がそんなヒット作を書けるなんて，すごいですね。

D **Summary Practice:** Fill in the blanks with suitable words beginning with the letters indicated. Then listen to the CD and check your answers.

DL 25 CD2-06

Dillon Helbig, an (1. **a**) (2. **a**), is in the news. Using a (3. **j**) given to him by his (4. **g**), the (5. **e**)-year-old wrote a book about himself, entitled *The* (6. ***A***) *of Dillon Helbig's Crismis*. Dillon (7. **l**) to see his book on the library (8. **s**) so that other (9. **c**) could read it. His solution? He snuck it onto the shelf of the (10. **A**) (11. **P**) (12. **L**). The (13. **l**) who found it read it to their own children, and decided to make it an (14. **o**) library book. And now, the book is a (15. **h**), with 64 names on the (16. **w**) (17. **l**). Dillon's (18. **p**) are proud of him for (19. **i**) other children and adults, and for (20. **b**) in himself.

E **Discussion:** Share your ideas and opinions with your classmates.

1. What was your favorite book when you were a child? Why did you like it?
2. Have you ever thought of writing a book? If you were going to write something, what kind of book would you like to write?
3. Look for information about other books written by young (child or teenage) authors.

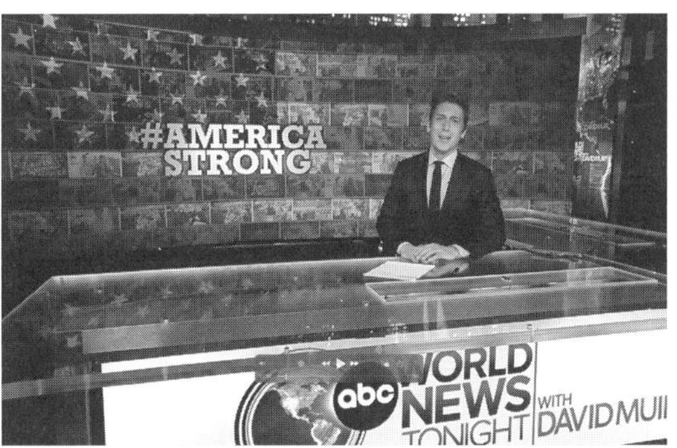

リンキング(連結)

英語では語尾が子音で終わる単語が多く，また，音節同士の結び付きが強いため，単語として独立していても語の境界を越えて２つ以上の単語が結び付いて発音されることがある。これをリンキング(linking)という。例えば，子音で終わる語と母音で始まる語といった２つの語が連続する場合，その子音と母音が結び付いて一つの音節のように発音される。基本的には，どのような子音と母音の組み合わせでも可能であるが，代表的な例としては，破裂音(p, t, d, k, gなど)と母音，摩擦音(f, v, θ, s, ʃなど)と母音，その他の子音(m, n, l, rなど)と母音の連結などがある。

—...***in‿need‿of‿a*** special touch. *(Volunteers in Loveland, P.10 L.4)*

—I guess you could say it's the ***kind‿of*** place where people wear their ***hearts‿on*** their sleeves... *(Volunteers in Loveland, P.10 L.8)*

—..., the animal care team constructing this sling ***out‿of‿a*** baby onesie, and some elastic straps. *(Penguin at Arizona Aquarium, P.21 L.8)*

—As ***part‿of‿one‿of*** the largest restoration efforts on the Upper Basin, ... *(Colorado River Most Endangered, P.29 L.27)*

—The Endurance, ***one‿of*** history's greatest shipwrecks, now finally found. *(Endurance Ship Found in Antarctica, P.47 L.4)*

—..., Disney, giving ABC News this exclusive first look at ***one‿of*** the masts. *(Endurance Ship Found in Antarctica, P.47 L.9)*

—Dillon Helbig ***took‿an‿old*** journal his grandmother gave him and ***turned‿it‿into‿an*** 82-page book, ... *(An Inspiring Child Author, P.53 L.7)*

—The library estimates that'll ***take‿about*** two years for everyone to ***sign‿it‿out***. *(An Inspiring Child Author, P.54 L.26)*

—***One‿of*** the species most vulnerable to a warming ocean. *(Saving the Galapagos, P.67 L.9)*

—And then I saw my kids, and I just ***lost‿it***. *(The Marathon Mom, P.75 L.24)*

—Retired and ***on‿a*** fixed income, those tough choices include asking for help. *(Rising Prices, P.80 L.12)*

—And no, the irony ***of‿a*** non-speaking autistic encouraging you to use your voice... *(Valedictorian Speech, P.93 L.18)*

Historic Gunmaker Settlement

The Gist
- What was the historic settlement reached with Remington Arms?
- What conditions led to the settlement being reached?

Before You Watch the News *Warm-up Exercises*

A Vocabulary Check: Choose the correct definition for each of the words below.

DL 26 CD2-07

1. claim ( )
2. landmark ( )
3. accountability ( )
4. fateful ( )
5. impressionable ( )

a. the condition of being responsible
b. having disastrous consequences
c. to state or declare
d. easily influenced; susceptible
e. marking a turning point or significant change

B Fill in the blanks with appropriate expressions from the Vocabulary Check above. Change the word forms where necessary.

1. It was Mark's ( ) decision to quit his job that led to the divorce.
2. Their lack of ( ) regarding the factory fire was disturbing.
3. Be careful what you say around Tommy. Children are very ( ).
4. Some students ( ) that they were not told about the deadline for the report.
5. In a ( ) deal, the two companies decided to merge and market their clothes to a wider audience.

Focus on the News Story

D. Muir: Now to the historic settlement this evening by a gunmaker, the first for a mass shooting in this country. Remington Arms now agreeing to pay $73 million to the families of some of the victims of the Sandy Hook Elementary School shooting, who claimed the company marketed the AR-15-style rifle 1. ______________________________ ______________________, sometimes in video games. One ad with a tagline that said, "Consider your man card reissued." Here's ABC's Janai Norman tonight.

J. Norman: The landmark lawsuit settlement, tonight, gun manufacturer Remington Arms agreeing to pay a historic $73 million to 2. ________ ______________________________ of the Sandy Hook Elementary School shooting.

V. De La Rosa, mother of Noah: Today is a day of accountability for an industry that has thus far enjoyed operating with immunity and impunity.

J. Norman: Those families suing Remington, maker of the Bushmaster semi-automatic rifle 3. ______________________________, accusing the company of unethically advertising a weapon meant for war to young men, including product placement in video games, and ads like this one, reading, "Consider your man card reissued." Remington had previously denied responsibility, but had no comment today.

N. Hockley, mother of Dylan: It was designed to kill, quickly and efficiently. The Sandy Hook shooter helped fulfill that purpose, shooting 154 bullets in less than five minutes and killing 26 innocent people, 4. ____.

J. Norman: Today, more than nine years after that fateful morning, the pain is still raw.

F. Wheeler, mother of Ben: True justice would be our 15-year-old healthy and standing next to us, right now. But Benny will never be 15.

J. Norman: I sat down with Francine and David Wheeler, who said they joined the lawsuit 5. ____ ________________ after losing their six-year-old son, Ben.

Why did you decide not knowing how long it would take, how painful it could be?

D. Wheeler, father of Ben: It made sense to us, as people, to take part in this, to try to do something, to make it so that another dad doesn't have to stand here and deal with this. How could you not 6. __________ ____ to try and change something?

F. Wheeler: We're not done being parents to Benjamin.

D. Wheeler: No. Not by a long shot. And today is... is... is an... is an example of that.

J. Norman: And, David, the families saying today, this is not about the money. This is about change. They wouldn't settle without Remington agreeing to release thousands of pages of internal documents that the families say show Remington marketed their guns to get them in the hands of impressionable, violent-prone young men like the one [7.] ______________________________ in an elementary school here in Newtown. David?

D. Muir: And just incredible to think all of those children would now be 15 and 16 years old. Janai Norman, tonight. Thank you.

Notes

L.2 **Remington Arms** 「レミントン・アームズ社〈アメリカの老舗銃器メーカー〉」

L.3 **Sandy Hook Elementary School shooting** 「サンディフック小学校銃乱射事件〈2012年12月14日コネチカット州のサンディフック小学校で発生した銃乱射事件で，生徒20名と職員6名が犠牲となった〉」

L.5 **AR-15-style rifle** 「AR-15スタイル・ライフル〈軽量の半自動小銃で殺傷能力が高いとされる〉」

L.7 **Consider your man card reissued.** 「あなたのマンカード［男証明書］を再発行しましょう〈男らしさをアピールしようとしたキャッチフレーズで，若い男性を標的に銃を所持することを勧めている〉」

L.14 **with immunity and impunity** 「罰を受けず起訴もされずに」

L.15 **Bushmaster semi-automatic rifle** 「ブッシュマスター半自動（セミオートマチック）ライフル〈ブッシュマスター社が製造するライフルで，引き金を引いて銃弾を発射した後に，自動的に薬きょうを排出し，次の銃弾が装填されるもの〉」

L.18 **product placement** 「プロダクト・プレイスメント〈商品の露出を高める広告手法のこと。レミントン社はビデオゲームの小道具として実在の商品を出したり，ゲーム内の背景に商品名を載せたりするなどして，銃の販売促進をしたとされている〉」

L.41 **Not by a long shot** 「全くそんなことはありません；ベンの親としての役割はまだまだ終わりません」

L.47 **violent-prone** 「暴力的な傾向がある〈文法的にはviolence-proneが正しい〉」

Background of the News

アメリカ国内には，人口（約３億3000万人）より多い４億丁以上の銃が流通していると推定され，自殺を除き，年間で１万数千人が銃で亡くなるという。なかでも，学校における銃乱射事件が後を絶たない。最近では，2022年５月に南部テキサス州ユバルディ（Uvalde）の小学校で事件が起きた。18歳の男が教室に侵入し，殺傷能力の高い半自動（semi-automatic）ライフル銃AR-15スタイル・ライフル（AR-15-style rifle）を乱射した。

2012年12月14日，コネティカット（Connecticut）州ニュータウン（Newtown）のサンディフック小学校（Sandy Hook Elementary School）で銃乱射事件が発生した。地元に住む当時20歳の男は，小学校での乱射前に母親も銃殺していた。男は，小学校の窓ガラスを割って侵入し，銃を乱射。6～7歳の児童20人を含む26人が犠牲となった。乱射後に男は校舎内で自殺しているのが発見されたが，米司法当局は動機などが解明できないまま捜査を終了している。本ニュースストーリーで紹介されているように，この事件の犯行に使われた銃のメーカー（gun manufacturer）側と遺族が2022年２月15日，和解することで合意した。遺族に7300万ドル（約84億円）が支払われたが，こうした和解は異例だという。

乱射事件が起きるたびに銃規制が議論になるものの，「人を殺すのは人であって銃ではない」というスローガンを掲げて銃保有の権利を主張する全米ライフル協会（NRA）の共和党への影響力が大きく，これまで銃規制は進んでいなかった。また，銃所持の権利は合衆国憲法修正第２条で保障されている。しかし，最近になってようやく銃規制に向ける動きが出てきた。2022年６月25日に，21歳未満の購入者の身元確認を厳しくすることなどが盛り込まれた法案が連邦議会で可決され，バイデン大統領が署名して銃規制強化法が成立した。銃規制に対する本格的な法制定は28年ぶりとなった。

After You Watch the News　*Exercises*

A Listen to the news story and fill in the blanks in the text.

CD2-08 [Normal]　CD2-09 [Slow]

B **Multiple Choice Questions:** Select the best answer to each question.

1. Remington Arms is being sued
   a. for encouraging young men to go to war.
   b. by the victims of a mass shooting at an elementary school.
   c. because of their marketing strategies for the weapons used in a mass shooting.

2. The shooting at Sandy Hook Elementary School
   a. took place just over ten years ago.
   b. resulted in the deaths of 26 15-year-olds.
   c. was carried out in just minutes by one person.

3. The families involved in the lawsuit
   a. have been accused by some people of being unethical.
   b. insisted that Remington Arms turn over thousands of their documents.
   c. look forward to receiving a large amount of money to compensate for their loss.

4. The marketing of the AR-15 rifles by Remington Arms
   a. is criticized for targeting impressionable young men.
   b. encouraged young men to be more ethical.
   c. was exclusively carried out through video games.

C Translate the following Japanese into English. Then listen to the CD and practice the conversation with your partner. DL 27 CD2-10

A: They did it! Remington Arms has agreed to pay millions to the Sandy Hook families.

B: Incredible! 1. ______________________________.

A: That's right. The weapons industry has gotten away with too much for too long.

B: It won't bring those beautiful children back, though.

A: 2. That kind of true justice is impossible but now, ______________________________.

B: 3. ______________________________.

A: It's a historic step, to be sure.

1. 説明責任を果たすべき時がついに来たのです。
2. そういう真の正義は不可能ですが，子どもを失うという恐ろしい苦しみを経験しなければならない親は少なくなるかもしれません。
3. ９年かかりましたが，これが大きな変化の始まりになることを期待しましょう。

D **Summary Practice:** Fill in the blanks with suitable words beginning with the letters indicated. Then listen to the CD and check your answers.

DL 28 CD2-11

Nine years ago, Sandy Hook (1. **E**) (2. **S**) was the scene of one of the deadliest (3. **m**) (4. **s**) in U.S. history, claiming the lives of (5. **t**)-(6. **s**) people, including many innocent children. The shooter's (7. **w**) was an AR-15-style (8. **s**)-(9. **a**) rifle, designed to (10. **k**) quickly. Today, in a (11. **l**) (12. **l**) settlement, the company that manufactured the gun has agreed to pay $73 million to the (13. **f**) of (14. **n**) victims of that shooting. In a (15. **h**) first, (16. **R**) (17. **A**) was accused of (18. **m**) a weapon intended for (19. **w**) to young males, often placing ads in (20. **v**) (21. **g**). As part of the deal, Remington will release (22. **i**) (23. **d**) that will help show that their guns were marketed to (24. **i**) young men prone to (25. **v**). For the families, it has been a long, tough struggle, but their actions will hopefully lead to (26. **c**).

E **Discussion:** Share your ideas and opinions with your classmates.

1. Mass shootings continue to be a huge problem in the U.S. Check the statistics on the number of mass shootings and the number of people who lost their lives in mass shootings since the start of this year. Have gun laws changed in the past five years?
2. What are the laws regarding gun ownership in Japan? Why do you think the situation is so different from the U.S.?
3. New Zealand, Ireland and Australia are three other countries that have experienced mass shootings in the past. Choose one of these countries and research how they dealt with the problems. How did the laws change after the shootings?

News Story

10

Air Date: February 21, 2022
Duration: 2'08"

Saving the Galapagos

The Gist

- What do the scientists want people to know about the Galapagos Islands?
- What have they discovered there?

Before You Watch the News *Warm-up Exercises*

A Vocabulary Check: Choose the correct definition for each of the words below.

DL 29 CD2-12

1. stunning ( ) a. to observe and check over a period of time
2. vulnerable ( ) b. unsafe; susceptible to danger or harm
3. starvation ( ) c. unspoiled; in perfect condition
4. monitor ( ) d. a weak condition or death due to a lack of food
5. pristine ( ) e. extremely attractive

B Fill in the blanks with appropriate expressions from the Vocabulary Check above. Change the word forms where necessary.

1. The diamond was in ( ) condition, so it sold for a high price.
2. The proposed law will harm the most ( ) members of the community by blocking financial aid.
3. Wow, Kelly! You look ( ) in that red dress.
4. It's important to ( ) the fashion trends of teens if you want the business to succeed.
5. The government fears widespread ( ) if the draught continues.

Focus on the News Story

D. Muir: Finally tonight here, our team, traveling the world. Amy Robach with the scientists saving some of the most beautiful creatures on Earth in the Galapagos Islands.

A. Robach: Tonight, the stunning beauty of the Galapagos Islands and what scientists want you to urgently know about 1. ______________________________. First, I come face-to-face with baby sea lions.

Oh, my God. This is so cool.

One of the species most vulnerable to a warming ocean. Life here is dependent on cold water. And currents bring nutrient-rich cold water from Antarctica. But 2. ______________________, that cold water doesn't make it to the surface, and without those nutrients, fish and algae die off and animals that feed on them face starvation. Back on land, we hike to find marine iguanas. Their population, scientists say, are now becoming a barometer of climate change.

J. Aguas, naturalist, Lindblad Expeditions: They are perfect environmental indicators. They can tell you how healthy an environment is 3. ______________________________. They specialize in only feeding on green algae. But there's a problem, with the water becoming warmer, the green algae disappears.

A. Robach: Ninety-six percent of the Galapagos Islands are protected by Ecuador's Galapagos Marine Reserve and closely monitored to help conserve the natural habitat.

4. ____?

C. Romero, expedition leader, Lindblad Expeditions: Most of the populations, we have reduced numbers. And this is why it's so important to maintain the Galapagos as a national park, as a protected area. Because when animals are considered endangered, it's because they cannot reproduce well, or their habitats are very reduced.

D. Muir: And so, let's bring in Amy Robach from the Galapagos Islands, tonight. And, Amy, I know you're witnessing firsthand 5. ____, the most vulnerable species there. And I know there's really an urgent effort to protect it all.

A. Robach: That's right, David. We have been in awe witnessing the unique wildlife and the pristine conditions here in the Galapagos Islands alongside naturalists, who work tirelessly to make sure things stay that way. In fact, 6. ____ expanding the Galapagos Marine Reserve by more than 23,000 square miles, David.

D. Muir: A powerful move. Thank you, Amy. We'll be watching *GMA* first thing in the morning. Good night.

Notes L.3 **the Galapagos Islands** 「ガラパゴス諸島〈「ガラパゴ」はスペイン語で「ゾウガメ」という意味。東太平洋の赤道直下に位置するエクアドル領の諸島。外界と孤絶し，ゾウガメやイグアナなど島独自の進化した生物が生息している〉」

L.12 **make it to ~** 「～に達する；～へ到達する；～までたどり着く」

L.13 **algae** 「藻（類）」

L.14 **marine iguanas** 「ウミイグアナ〈ガラパゴス諸島の海岸に群生し海藻を食べるトカゲ〉」

L.17 **naturalist** 「動物学者」

L.17 **Lindblad Expeditions** 「リンドブラッド・エクスペディションズ社〈航海と環境教育を組み合わせた旅を企画するクルーズ旅行会社で，科学調査に参加するツアーなどを提案している〉」

L.20 **green algae** 「緑藻類」

L.23 **Ecuador** 「エクアドル共和国〈= Republic of Ecuador 南米北西部の共和国〉」

L.23 **Galapagos Marine Reserve** 「ガラパゴス海洋保護区〈ガラパゴス諸島とその周辺の水域。世界最大級の海洋保護区で，世界自然遺産にも登録されている〉」

L.36 **in awe** 「畏敬の念を抱いて；畏怖の念を感じつつ」

L.42 ***GMA*** 「= *Good Morning America*〈ABC で放送されている朝の情報番組〉」

After You Watch the News — *Exercises*

A Listen to the news story and fill in the blanks in the text.

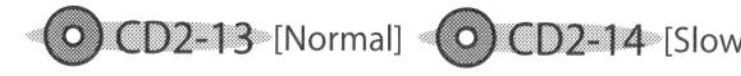

B **Multiple Choice Questions:** Select the best answer to each question.

1. Which of the following is ***NOT*** mentioned as a way of protecting the varied species in the Galapagos Islands?
   a. expanding the area of the protected reserve
   b. installing barometers in the water around the islands
   c. monitoring the numbers of certain species of animals

2. The Galapagos Marine Reserve
   a. has recently become a popular tourist site.
   b. covers 23,000 square miles of the Galapagos Islands.
   c. is controlled by the government of Ecuador.

3. Marine iguanas
   a. can only live in cold water.
   b. produce green algae when the water is warm.
   c. are helping scientists determine the condition of their habitat.

4. Which of the following statements is true regarding the water surrounding the Galapagos Islands?
   a. It eventually flows up to Antarctica.
   b. As it warms, the cold water stays beneath the surface.
   c. Scientists are finding that it contains more nutrients than before.

C Translate the following Japanese into English. Then listen to the CD and practice the conversation with your partner.

DL 30 CD2-15

A: Look at those baby sea lions! I've never seen them up close before.

B: 1. They're beautiful animals, ________________________________.

A: What do you mean? They look so strong and healthy.

B: It's all about the warming ocean. 2. ________________________________ ________________________________, so that's a problem for the animals that feed on them.

A: Like these sea lions?

B: That's right. 3. ________________________________ ____________________. The situation is urgent.

1. 美しい生き物ですが，最も弱い動物の一つでもあるのです。
2. 魚や藻類は冷たい海水に含まれる栄養分が必要で，それらがなければ生きていけないため，それを餌とする動物にとっては問題なのです。
3. 海水温が上がり続ければ，それら(アシカ)は飢餓に直面する可能性があります。

D **Summary Practice:** Fill in the blanks with suitable words beginning with the letters indicated. Then listen to the CD and check your answers.

DL 31 CD2-16

The ABC News team has traveled to the (1. G   ) Islands to investigate the effects of (2. c   ) (3. c   ). Amid the (4. s   ) beauty of these islands, scientists warn that the (5. w   ) oceans are an urgent problem. In spite of the fact that (6. n   )-(7. s   ) percent of the area is part of a (8. m   ) (9. r   ) established to (10. c   ) the natural (11. h   ), the populations of most (12. s   ) on the islands are getting smaller. The many (13. v   ) creatures must continue to be protected to keep them from becoming (14. e   ), defined as the inability to (15. r   ) well or a (16. r   ) habitat. The population of marine (17. i   ) is a good (18. b   ) of climate change, and the problems are apparent. Scientists, naturalists and the Ecuadorean (19. g   ) are working tirelessly to protect the unique (20. w   ) of these beautiful islands. Thanks to their hard work, the Galapagos Marine Reserve has been expanded by more than 23,000 square miles.

E **Discussion:** Share your ideas and opinions with your classmates.

1. How much do you know about the Galapagos Islands? Do an internet search and see what you can find out. What are some of the species unique to these islands? If you can, check out one of the YouTube videos introducing the amazing wildlife in this part of the world.

2. According to the news story, most animal populations in the Galapagos Islands are declining. What are some examples of endangered species in Japan? What is being done to protect them?

3. One reason for the expansion of the Marine Reserve is the problem of overfishing, which has become a major issue worldwide. See what you can find out about the current state of overfishing and the world's efforts to deal with it.

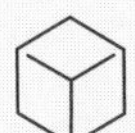

Useful Grammar from the News

無生物所有格

無生物の固有名詞や普通名詞に所有格の'sが付くことは，英語でよく見られるが，ニュース英語では，さらにその傾向が顕著である。例えば，最初の例文では，「アメリカの」を後置して"..., a day honoring march towards racial equality of America, ..."とするより，所有格の'sを使う方が端的になるため，話しことばとして伝わりやすくなる。特に場所，時，国名，地名を示す名詞に多く見られる。

—Tonight, Juneteenth, a day honoring ***America's*** march towards racial equality, ... (*Commemorating Juneteenth, P.15 L.7*)

—It is ***this region's*** adaptation to climate change. (*Colorado River Most Endangered, P.29 L.30*)

—Meantime back here at home tonight, and to ***Florida's*** controversial legislation passing. (*Controversial "Don't Say Gay" Bill, P.35 L.1*)

—Tonight, the remarkable discovery, nearly 10,000 feet below the surface at the bottom of ***Antarctica's*** Weddell Sea. (*Endurance Ship Found in Antarctica, P.47 L.3*)

—The Endurance, one of ***history's*** greatest shipwrecks, now finally found. (*Endurance Ship Found in Antarctica, P.47 L.4*)

—Ninety-six percent of the Galapagos Islands are protected by ***Ecuador's*** Galapagos Marine Reserve... (*Saving the Galapagos, P.68 L.22*)

—Factors driving the price spikes include everything from ***Russia's*** invasion of Ukraine... (*Rising Prices, P.81 L.23*)

The Marathon Mom

The Gist
- Why did Keira D'Amato stop running and then start again?
- What is the message she wants to share?

Before You Watch the News — *Warm-up Exercises*

A Vocabulary Check: Choose the correct definition for each of the words below.

DL 32 CD2-17

1. temporarily	( )	**a.**	a period of ten years
2. ankle	( )	**b.**	for a limited period of time
3. stride	( )	**c.**	the way you walk or run
4. compete	( )	**d.**	the joint connecting the leg and the foot
5. decade	( )	**e.**	to try to win something by defeating others

B Fill in the blanks with appropriate expressions from the Vocabulary Check above. Change the word forms where necessary.

1. Have you heard which teams will be (   ) in the championship match?
2. It's hard to believe we've been working together for a (   ) already.
3. John's coach advised him to work on his (   ) if he wants to win races.
4. Kim has a broken (   ). She fell while she was ice skating.
5. That shop is closed (   ), but they plan to reopen in the fall.

Focus on the News Story

D. Muir: Finally tonight here, so many moms across this country working and raising children, so often forced to temporarily put dreams on hold. Tonight, here, the mom who decided it was time.

Tonight, in Richmond, Virginia, the mother of two who wants you to know [1.] ______________________________. And what she's now done, "America Strong." Thirty-seven-year-old Keira D'Amato started running at 13 years old. She ran in high school, in college, and then stopped after an ankle injury. She would later get her job, and then raise a family. But it was after her second child was born, she decided, "I want to run again." Slowly [2.] ______________________________ ____________________, her stride back, starting to compete again. And then, just days ago, competing in the Houston Marathon.

Relative: Go. Go, Keira!

D. Muir: And this is the moment.

Relative: Go. Go. Yeah!

D. Muir: Keira crossing the finish line: 2 hours, 19 minutes, 12 seconds, beating the previous record by 24 seconds, breaking the American record in the women's marathon. [3.] ______________________________ ____________________. And right here, tonight...

K. D'Amato, Runner: Hi, David.

D. Muir: ...Keira, on that moment, crossing the finish line, her children waiting for her.

K. D'Amato: It was just a roller coaster of emotions crossing that finish line. And then I saw my kids, and I just lost it. I had a decade where I was just a fan of running. And I sat there watching, just thinking, like, what if? What if I hadn't stopped? **4.** ______________________________ ______________________? What if I just gave a little bit more? And I finally found the answer to that "what if."

D. Muir: Tonight, Keira, and her hope.

K. D'Amato: To all of you out there that have your "what if," I guess my message to you is, uhm, you know, I'll share some of my courage with you, and hopefully you guys can find... find a way to go find "what if."

D. Muir: In fact, she's now setting her sights on the Summer Olympics 2024.

K. D'Amato: **5.** ____ ________________________. It feels just totally crazy that you invited me on, but I'm happy to be here. And good night, everybody.

D. Muir: We're cheering you on, Keira, right along with your kids. I hope to see you at the Olympics. I'm David Muir. I hope to see you right back here, tomorrow, in the meantime. Till then, good night.

Notes L.2 **put ~ on hold** 「～を中断する；～を保留する；～を自制する」
L.4 **Richmond** 「リッチモンド〈バージニア州の州都〉」
L.12 **Houston Marathon** 「ヒューストンマラソン〈1972年以来，テキサス州ヒューストンで毎年1月に開催されているマラソン大会〉」
L.23 **roller coaster of emotions** 「ジェットコースターに乗っているような（起伏の激しい）気持ち」
L.24 **I just lost it.** 「= I just lost control of my emotions（ゴールにいる子どもたちを見て）感動で胸がいっぱいになった」

After You Watch the News — *Exercises*

A Listen to the news story and fill in the blanks in the text.

CD2-18 [Normal] CD2-19 [Slow]

B **T/F Questions:** Mark the following sentences true (T) or false (F) according to the information in the news story.

( ) **1.** Keira D'Amato had a job and raised a family before starting to run.
( ) **2.** Keira was unable to run in high school because of a serious injury.
( ) **3.** Keira had to ride on a roller coaster as part of the Houston Marathon.
( ) **4.** Keira broke a record in the Houston Marathon, with her two children watching.
( ) **5.** Keira hopes that other people will find courage from hearing her story.
( ) **6.** Keira is hoping to participate in the Summer Olympics 2024.

C Translate the following Japanese into English. Then listen to the CD and practice the conversation with your partner. DL 33 CD2-20

A: Keira was thinking of running in the Houston Marathon last week. Did she do it?
B: [1.] Not only did she run, ______________________________
______________________________!
A: Wow! I knew back in college that she was going to do great things.
B: [2.] Don't you remember how heartbroken she was when ______________________________
______________________________?
A: Really! Then she got a great job and had a great family but she still wanted to run.
B: [3.] ______________________________,
but she never gave up.
A: Keira's a real winner!

1. 彼女は走っただけでなく，女子マラソンのアメリカ記録を破りました。
2. 足首を怪我して走るのをやめなければならなかったとき，彼女がどれだけ心を痛めていたか覚えていませんか。
3. 彼女は10年間，夢を中断しなければならなかったけれど，決してあきらめなかったのです。

D **Summary Practice:** Fill in the blanks with suitable words beginning with the letters indicated. Then listen to the CD and check your answers.

DL 34 CD2-21

Keira D'Amato, a (1. **t**)-(2. **s**)-year-old from (3. **V**), is in the news for beating the (4. **p**) record at the (5. **H**) (6. **M**) by (7. **t**)-(8. **f**) seconds. D'Amato, a (9. **m**) of two, began running at the age of 13 and enjoyed the sport through (10. **h**) school and (11. **c**). However, an (12. **a**) injury forced her to stop. For a (13. **d**) as she got a (14. **j**), married and had two (15. **c**), she was just a (16. **f**) of running, always wondering, "(17. **W**) (18. **i**)?" After the birth of her second child, D'Amato worked up the (19. **c**) to start again, slowly getting her (20. **s**) back and (21. **c**) again. With her (22. **s**) now on the 2024 (23. **s**) (24. **O**), the "Marathon Mom" hopes to inspire others to find the courage to follow their (25. **d**).

E **Discussion:** Share your ideas and opinions with your classmates.

1. How much do you know about marathons? Choose one of the major marathons listed below and see what you can learn about when and where it is held, when it started, who participates, and what sets it apart from other marathons.

   [The Boston Marathon / The New York City Marathon / The London Marathon]

2. Look for other stories about women who successfully fulfilled their dreams while raising children. Share your findings with your classmates.

単語のアクセント

日本語では「バナナ」という語の３つの音は，ほぼ同じ強さと長さで発音されるが，正しい英語の発音では，第２音節にアクセントが置かれ“banana” /bənǽnə/ のように３つの音節は弱・強・弱のリズムで発音される。また，アクセントのある音節は，ない音節より「強く」，「長く」ピッチも「高く」発音される。“banana”における各音節の強さと高さを黒丸の大きさとその位置で表すと●●●のようになる。聞き手に意図を正確に伝える上で，正しいアクセントで話すことはとても重要である。以下の語では，特にアクセントの位置に注意して発音する必要がある。なお，単語中の(´)の記号は強いアクセント(第１アクセント)を表し，(`)はそれに準ずる強さのアクセント(第２アクセント)を示している。

—..., ***vòluntéers*** in Loveland have been stamping and mailing out hundreds of thousands of ***Válentines***. *(Volunteers in Loveland, P.10 L.10)*

—I have to take them a grain of—with a grain of salt, but a ***màrgaríta*** on the side. *(Volunteers in Loveland, P.11 L.22)*

—In Ft. Worth, 95-year-old Opal Lee, a leading ***ádvocate*** of the holiday... *(Commemorating Juneteenth, P.15 L.19)*

—..., ***symbólic*** of the additional time it took for those in Galveston. *(Commemorating Juneteenth, P.16 L.23)*

—Tonight, an ***óminous*** new report from a conservation group, ... *(Colorado River Most Endangered, P.28 L.7)*

—..., threatening the environment, ***ágricùlture***, and reliable water supplies... *(Colorado River Most Endangered, P.28 L.12)*

—...who feel bullied or ***óstracìzed*** and have nowhere to turn. *(Controversial “Don’t Say Gay” Bill, P.36 L.26)*

—...schools ***ímplemènting*** it could lose access to federal grants due to a 1972 law. *(Controversial “Don’t Say Gay” Bill, P.36 L.33)*

—I hope to see you at the ***Olýmpics***. *(The Marathon Mom, P.75 L.38)*

Rising Prices

The Gist
- What is the current state of the U.S. economy?
- What are the reasons for this?

Before You Watch the News *Warm-up Exercises*

A Vocabulary Check: Choose the correct definition for each of the words below.

DL 35 CD2-22

1. essentials ( )
2. startling ( )
3. fixed ( )
4. reel ( )
5. spike ( )

a. a sharp increase
b. shocking; very surprising
c. to lose one's balance or falter; to be upset due to a shock
d. stable; set
e. necessities; basic things that are needed

B Fill in the blanks with appropriate expressions from the Vocabulary Check above. Change the word forms where necessary.

1. With the ( ) in tuition fees, Jake has to get a job if he wants to continue his education.
2. You can only take one small suitcase. Just pack the bare ( ).
3. The ( ) price lunch menu at that restaurant is a good bargain.
4. It was ( ) when the fire alarm accidently went off in the middle of the night.
5. Many people in the community are ( ) from the sudden change in policy.

Focus on the News Story

D. Muir: The war in Ukraine putting increasing pressure on the global economy. And here at home, the new numbers tonight, inflation now at the highest level since 1981.

Consumer prices up 8.5 percent over the past year. Energy prices up an eye-popping 32 percent.

Americans now paying $325 more per month just for the essentials than [1.] ____ ________. ABC's Mireya Villarreal is in Texas tonight.

M. Villarreal: Tonight, those startling numbers from the government, confirming what Mary Beth Snyder is struggling with, right now.

M. B. Snyder: Everybody is making tough choices.

M. Villarreal: Retired and on a fixed income, those tough choices include asking for help. This food bank outside Dallas providing her with groceries she just can't afford.

M. B. Snyder: It's very humbling to be on the receiving end [2.] ____________ ____.

M. Villarreal: With inflation at an eye-watering 8.5 percent, families across the country reeling from the fastest rise in prices since the Reagan administration.

M. Zandi, Chief Economist, Moody's Analytics: People are paying $325 per month more now, compared to a year ago, [3.] ______________________ ______________________________________.

M. Villarreal: Factors driving the price spikes include everything from Russia's invasion of Ukraine to supply chain snafus. Record gas prices a huge factor in inflation, too. And in an effort to bring them down, President Biden announced an emergency waiver to allow some gas stations to sell a higher blend of ethanol gas called E-15 during the summer.

President J. Biden: But here's what it means. E-15 is about 10 cents a gallon cheaper than E-10. But it's not gonna solve all our problems, but it's gonna help some people, and I'm committed to do [4.] ______________ ______________________.

M. Villarreal: David, it's worth noting that Biden's move only affects about two percent of the gas stations nationwide, so it's unclear how much this will actually help. Meanwhile, here at the North Texas Food Bank, they say March was their busiest month in about a year. And they say it's directly attributed to inflation. They fear [5.] _______________ ______________________. David?

Notes

L.13 **food bank** 「フード・バンク，食糧銀行〈困窮者支援のために食料を配給する民間の組織や施設〉」
L.13 **Dallas** 「ダラス〈テキサス州北東部の都市〉」
L.15 **on the receiving end** 「受ける［受け取る］側で」
L.18 **Reagan administration** 「レーガン政権〈米国第40代大統領として1981年1月から1989年1月まで政権についた。1982年9月には40年ぶりに失業率が10%を超え，深刻な不況下にあった〉」
L.20 **Chief Economist, Moody's Analytics** 「ムーディーズ・アナリティックス社，チーフ（首席）エコノミスト〈経済分析を専門とする企業で，さまざまな資産に関するデータを保有している〉」
L.24 **supply chain snafus** 「サプライチェーンの混乱〈サプライチェーンとは，製品が原材料の調達から，生産・物流・販売を経て，消費者の手に届くまでの全過程のこと〉」
L.26 **emergency waiver** 「緊急措置としての（規制）解除」
L.27 **E-15** 「イー・フィフティーン〈エタノールを最大15%含む混合ガソリン。スモッグの原因になるとして，E-15の夏季の販売を原則禁止としているが，ガソリン価格の高騰を受け，通年販売が許可された〉」

Background of the News

米国ではインフレが加速しており，特にエネルギーや食品を中心に値上がりが続いている。2022年7月14日付の『朝日新聞』によると，食費は前年同月比10.4%増，ガソリン代は59.9%増，ガス代は38.4%増，住居費は5.6%増と，切り詰めが難しい生活必需品(essentials)の費目での上昇が相次ぎ，米国民の家計を圧迫しているという。物価高は，サプライチェーンの混乱(supply chain snafus)による品薄や，ウクライナにおける戦争(the war in Ukraine)などが背景にあるとみられている。

インフレで価格が上がりすぎたことで，米国民が消費を控え始めた可能性があり，景気への悪影響は必至である。実際，2022年7月23日付の『日本経済新聞』によると，7月の米国の購買担当者景気指数は総合指数が47.5となり，好不況の分かれ目となる50を下回った。これは，新型コロナウイルスの感染拡大で経済活動が停滞していた2020年以来の低水準だという。

After You Watch the News　*Exercises*

A Listen to the news story and fill in the blanks in the text.

CD2-23 [Normal]　CD2-24 [Slow]

B **Multiple Choice Questions:** Select the best answer to each question.

1. The current level of inflation in the U.S.
   a. is the highest it has ever been.
   b. is due exclusively to the situation in Ukraine.
   c. shows a higher increase in energy prices than in consumer prices.

2. Which statement describes the current situation of many Americans?
   a. Their energy prices have doubled in the past year.
   b. They are dealing with the fastest spike in prices in 40 years.
   c. They paid $325 more for essentials than they did in the previous month.

3. Mary Beth Snyder
   a. made the tough choice to live on a fixed income.
   b. has given help to people in need and received help from others.
   c. cannot afford to buy groceries because she had to retire.

4. Which statement is ***NOT*** true regarding President Biden's emergency waiver?
   a. It may result in a supply chain snafu.
   b. He is asking gas stations to make a change.
   c. It will only affect a small percentage of gas stations in the U.S.

C Translate the following Japanese into English. Then listen to the CD and practice the conversation with your partner. DL 36 CD2-25

A: Look at this grocery bill! 1. ____
________________________________.

B: Really! I paid almost $3.00 for a loaf of bread yesterday. It's crazy.

A: 2. ____.

B: Actually, I saw him at the food bank last week.

A: Wow. He always donated food there when he was still working.

B: 3. And now ____. It must be tough.

A: Inflation has really gotten out of hand. I hope the president can find a way to stop it.

1. 去年より，生活必需品の支払いがかなり増えています。
2. 定収入で暮らしているラリーはどうしているのでしょうね。
3. そして今，彼は受け取る側になっているのです。

D Summary Practice: Fill in the blanks with suitable words beginning with the letters indicated. Then listen to the CD and check your answers.

DL 37 CD2-26

Americans from coast to coast are (1. r) as the country faces the worst (2. i) since 1981. With (3. c) prices up over (4. e) percent in just one year, people find themselves paying $325 more every month just for the (5. e). What is driving the price (6. s)? While there are numerous (7. f), the (8. w) in (9. U) and (10. s) (11. c) (12. s) are believed to be a big part. President Biden has proposed an (13. e) (14. w) that would allow gas stations to sell a higher (15. b) of ethanol gas during the (16. s) months. Experts note, however, that that will effect only (17. t) percent of gas stations around the country. In the meantime, (18. f) (19. b) are helping to provide more people than ever with the (20. g) they need.

E Discussion: Share your ideas and opinions with your classmates.

1. How is the economic situation of Japan at the moment? Has the war in Ukraine and the resulting supply chain problem had a negative impact on prices in this country, like in the U.S.?

2. Food banks are mentioned in the news story as being one source of support for people who are struggling to pay for groceries. Does Japan have food banks? See what you can find out about food banks in your area. Might you be interested in volunteering?

News Story **13**

Air Date: January 27, 2022
Duration: 2'34"

International Holocaust Remembrance Day

The Gist

- What happened at Auschwitz 75 years ago?
- Why did the Auschwitz survivors decide to return?

Before You Watch the News — *Warm-up Exercises*

A Vocabulary Check: Choose the correct definition for each of the words below.

DL 38 CD2-27

1. survivor ( )
2. perilous ( )
3. unchecked ( )
4. atrocities ( )
5. bond ( )

a. unrestrained; free to continue
b. very dangerous
c. connection; relationship
d. violent crimes; acts of cruelty
e. someone who remains alive despite severe hardship

B Fill in the blanks with appropriate expressions from the Vocabulary Check above. Change the word forms where necessary.

1. Realizing that the dark clouds signaled ( ) conditions ahead, the ship's captain headed back to shore.
2. If gas prices continue to rise ( ), we may have to sell our car.
3. Miraculously, there were over 100 ( ) from the plane crash.
4. It's unusual for a dog and a cat to have such a close ( ), but our pets really love each other.
5. After reading about the ( ) taking place in the region, we changed our travel plans.

Focus on the News Story

D. Muir: On this International Holocaust Remembrance Day, the survivors you met here.

It was a long and painful journey, 75 years later. The children of Auschwitz, the survivors, going back. They told us they believed it was their duty to remind the world how perilous unchecked hate can be. We were with them, [1.] ______________________________.

Airline staff: Enjoy your flight.

Holocaust survivor: Thank you, ma'am.

D. Muir: Then, the bus in Poland, one hour to Auschwitz. We were there as they slowly walked through that gate, the survivors whom we have documented for years.

Tova.

T. Friedman, Holocaust survivor: Oh, hi.

D. Muir: We will never forget Tova Friedman, putting to words [2.] ______________________________.

T. Friedman: That we didn't forget them. That I remember the little girl going

into the crematorium, and she wouldn't come back, that I played with.

D. Muir: You remember them.

T. Friedman: We remember. That's what it is. We remember.

D. Muir: There was David Marks, who had never gone back.

D. Marks, Holocaust survivor: But now, it's, ...I'm getting, ...I'm in the fourth quarter of my life.

D. Muir: [3.] ____ ______________, Kathy, he rarely talked about what had happened to him. But at 91, he told me while there, now, it's different.

D. Marks: They should know what happened. They should know that, never again.

T. Friedman: I remember walking in cold.

D. Muir: It was Tova who bravely went inside the crematorium. She told us why that day, saying it's important that [4.] ____________________ ______________________________________. She asked her daughter-in-law Sara to go in, as well.

T. Friedman: Go inside. Go all the way—

Daughter-in-law: Okay.

D. Muir: And tonight, two years later, she tells us she heard from so many of you, moved by that journey. And now, her hope.

T. Friedman: David, I hope that today, January 27th, will be remembered, not only with my generations, but [5.] ______________________________ ________________, so we don't forget the atrocities, and we honor those who aren't with us and have no name.

D. Muir: And David Marks, who shared his story with us two years ago after waiting so long to talk about it, we've learned he's now married to the woman who was right there by his side, Kathy, [6.] ____________ ____.

A powerful bond and a painful chapter they say we must never forget.

We'll never forget. Good night.

Notes

L.1 **International Holocaust Remembrance Day** 「国際ホロコースト記念日〈1月27日はアウシュビッツ強制収容所が当時のソ連軍によって解放された日〉」

L.4 **Auschwitz** 「アウシュビッツ強制収容所〈第2次大戦時に，ナチス・ドイツが当時占領下のポーランドに作った最大規模の強制収容所〉」

L.15 **putting to words** 「～を言葉で表す」

L.18 **crematorium** 「火葬場；遺体焼却炉」

L.22 **who had never gone back** 「彼は（2年前に企画された旅行まで一度もアウシュビッツに）戻ったことがなかった」

L.40 **my generations** 「= my generation〈文法的には単数の generation になる〉」

L.47 **painful chapter** 「つらい（人生の）一幕［出来事］」

Background of the News

1940年，アウシュビッツ (Auschwitz) 強制収容所は占領下のポーランド南部につくられ，後にナチス・ドイツ最大の収容所となった。第２次大戦中，ナチスは欧州各地から移送されてきたユダヤ人らに強制労働を課し，一度に大量の人々を殺す「ガス室」に送るなどして約110万人が犠牲になった。1945年１月，収容所に残されていた約7,500人が旧ソ連軍によって解放され，現在，アウシュビッツ強制収容所は博物館となっている。

2020年１月28日付の『朝日新聞』によると，アウシュビッツ博物館への訪問者は年々増え，2019年は過去最多の232万人を記録した。特に学校単位などで，若者らが見学するスタディーツアーの参加者は前年より２割増えたという。

本ニュースストーリーで紹介されているフリードマン (Friedman) さんのように，ホロコースト (the Holocaust) を生き延びた元収容者たちは，「ここで何が起こったかを世界に伝えることが自分の義務だ」との思いが強い。アウシュビッツの解放から80年近くが経過して生存者の高齢化が進んでいるものの，講演をオンライン配信したりAIの技術を用いてリアルタイムで生存者と会話ができる取り組みに参加したりするなど，多くの生存者が自身の体験を後世に伝える活動をしている。

After You Watch the News　*Exercises*

A Listen to the news story and fill in the blanks in the text.

B **Multiple Choice Questions:** Select the best answer to each question.

1. International Holocaust Remembrance Day aims to
   a. increase tourism to Poland.
   b. help people forget what happened at Auschwitz.
   c. insure that people today and in future generations remember what happened.

2. Which statement is ***NOT*** true about Tova Friedman?
   a. Her childhood friend was killed in the crematorium.
   b. Until recently, she was unable to speak about Auschwitz.
   c. She wants to honor those people who did not survive Auschwitz.

3. ABC News
   a. started International Holocaust Remembrance Day 75 years ago.
   b. has been documenting and reporting on the survivors' stories for years.
   c. has been trying to put Auschwitz survivors in touch with their relatives.

4. David Marks
   a. changed his mind about going back to visit Poland.
   b. married a woman that he knew while at Auschwitz.
   c. has talked frequently about his Auschwitz experience for over 70 years.

C Translate the following Japanese into English. Then listen to the CD and practice the conversation with your partner. DL 39 CD2-30

A: Sara, are you really going to Poland with your mother-in-law?

B: Of course. She asked me to, so I will join her.

A: 1. ______________________________.

B: She *is* brave! 2. But like many of the children of Auschwitz, ______________________________...

A: The world needs to know.

B: ...and to honor those people who didn't survive.

A: Tova is a strong woman. 3. ______________________________.

1. そこで起きた残虐な行為の後にそこへ戻るなんて，彼女はとても勇敢ですね。
2. でも，多くのアウシュビッツの子どもたちと同じように，彼女は何が起こったかを世界に伝えることが自分の義務だと信じています。
3. 彼女のような人がいるからこそ，私たちはこのようなことが二度と起こらないことを望むことができるのです。

D Summary Practice: Fill in the blanks with suitable words beginning with the letters indicated. Then listen to the CD and check your answers.

DL 40 CD2-31

Tova Friedman and David Marks are two Holocaust (1. **s**) of (2. **A**) who shared their stories with ABC News and with the world. On International Holocaust (3. **R**) (4. **D**), they spoke with David Muir about the terrible (5. **a**) that occurred there and the need to (6. **r**). Two years ago, Tova returned to (7. **P**) and walked all the way inside the (8. **c**) with her (9. **d**)-in-law. During the war, she saw a little (10. **g**) she (11. **p**) with go inside, and never come back. David Marks, at (12. **n**)-(13. **o**) years old, also decided it was time to make the (14. **p**) journey back. He was accompanied by his (15. **l**) (16. **p**), whom he later married. The survivors hope that (17. **J**) 27th will be a day that reminds future (18. **g**) how (19. **p**) unchecked (20. **h**) can be.

E Discussion: Share your ideas and opinions with your classmates.

1. How much do you know about the Holocaust? Do an internet search. Share your findings with the class.
2. *The Diary of Anne Frank* is a famous story of one young girl's experience during World War II. How is her story different from that of the Auschwitz survivors?
3. Do you know anyone who lived through World War II? Look for books and articles about stories of survivors from that time. What hardships did they face?

News Story
14

Air Date: May 10, 2022
Duration: 1'57"

Valedictorian Speech

The Gist
- What is special about Elizabeth Bonker's commencement speech?
- What is her message to her fellow graduates?

Before You Watch the News — *Warm-up Exercises*

A Vocabulary Check: Choose the correct definition for each of the words below.

DL 41 CD2-32

1. valedictorian	( )	a.	extremely happy; overjoyed
2. commencement	( )	b.	the graduating student with the highest grades, who gives a speech at graduation
3. elated	( )	c.	to identify an illness through tests
4. sibling	( )	d.	a brother or sister
5. diagnose	( )	e.	graduation ceremony

B Fill in the blanks with appropriate expressions from the Vocabulary Check above. Change the word forms where necessary.

1. I heard your brother is this year's ( ). You must feel so proud!
2. You have four ( )? What a big family!
3. Mr. Jones had to take some time off when he was ( ) with a serious heart problem.
4. Jenna was ( ) to learn she was going to become a grandmother.
5. There will be a performance of classical music before the ( ) begins.

Focus on the News Story

D. Muir: Finally tonight here, "America Strong." The valedictorian and the speech we won't soon forget.

Tonight, in Winter Park, Florida, a commencement speech like no other. It is definitely "America Strong."

E. Bonker, Valedictorian: Greetings to my fellow members of the elated class of 2022 and to the relieved parents, cheering siblings and [1.] ______________________.

D. Muir: Valedictorian Elizabeth Bonker delivering the commencement address to her class at Rollins College without speaking a word.

E. Bonker: Today, we celebrate our shared achievements. I know something about shared achievements, because I am affected by a form of autism [2.] ______________________.

D. Muir: Elizabeth was diagnosed with autism. She is nonverbal, but it hasn't stopped her. Going to school, learning and communicating in her own way. Using her finger to point to letters one by one, [3.] ______________________. Finding her voice with computer-generated, text-to-speech technology.

E. Bonker: God gave you a voice. Use it. And no, the irony of a non-speaking autistic encouraging you to use your voice is not lost on me. Because

if you can see the worth in me, then you can see the worth 4. ______________________________.

D. Muir: Elizabeth graduating with a 4.0, majoring in Social Innovation and a minor in English. And right here, tonight...

E. Bonker: Hi, David.

D. Muir: Elizabeth, the valedictorian.

E. Bonker: We cannot speak, but we can hear, feel, and think. Just like the deaf use sign language, non-speakers who learn to type will no longer suffer in silence.

D. Muir: And tonight, here, Elizabeth 5. ______________________________.

E. Bonker: Sometimes, it is the people no one imagines anything of who do the things no one can imagine. Be those people. Be the light.

D. Muir: Be the light. Elizabeth certainly is that, and we celebrate you. I'm David Muir. I hope to see you right back here, tomorrow night. From all of us here, good night.

Notes
L.3 **Winter Park** 「ウィンターパーク〈フロリダ州中東部の都市〉」
L.9 **Rollins College** 「ロリンズ・カレッジ〈フロリダ州ウィンターパークにある1885年に創設された私立大学で約30の学部課程（major）を有する〉」
L.17 **text-to-speech technology** 「テキスト読み上げ［音声変換］技術」
L.19 **not lost on me** 「自分なりに（意味が）理解できる［分かる］」
L.22 **with a 4.0** 「大学成績評価（GPA）4.0点の成績〈成績証明書の学業成績を平均点で換算した数値をGPA（Grade Point Average）という。アメリカの成績評価法は，主に5段階評価（A=4.0, B=3.0, C=2.0, D=1.0, F=0）で行われており，ボンカーさんはオールAの成績を収めたことがわかる〉」
L.23 **minor** 「副専攻〈アメリカの大学では，「主専攻」（major）の必修科目以外に，ある特定分野の科目を一定数以上取得すると，卒業時に「副専攻」（minor）として認定される〉」

After You Watch the News *Exercises*

A Listen to the news story and fill in the blanks in the text.

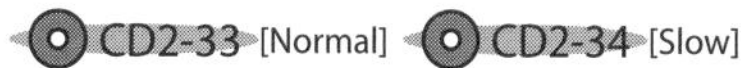

B **T/F Questions:** Mark the following sentences true (T) or false (F) according to the information in the news story.

(　　) **1.** Elizabeth Bonker was named valedictorian because she is autistic.
(　　) **2.** The valedictorian delivered her speech to the graduates of Rollins College as well as their families and friends.
(　　) **3.** Although she is nonverbal, Elizabeth can communicate using her fingers and technology.
(　　) **4.** Elizabeth majored in Social Innovation while at the university.
(　　) **5.** People who are deaf can communicate only by typing.
(　　) **6.** In her speech, Elizabeth urged her classmates to use the voices God gave them.

C Translate the following Japanese into English. Then listen to the CD and practice the conversation with your partner.

DL 42 CD2-35

A: Did you hear about the commencement ceremony?

B: No. How was it?

A: 1. Well, graduations are always dramatic, but ______________________________

______________________________.

B: What makes you say that?

A: 2. ______________________________.

B: You mean she can't talk? How could she make a speech?

A: 3. ______________________________

______________________________.

B: That's amazing.

A: And she is amazing! She gave everyone a lot to think about.

1. さて，卒業式はいつもドラマチックですが，今年の（卒業式）はすぐには忘れがたいものになりました。
2. 卒業生総代は，一種の自閉症で，そのために言葉が話せなかったのです。
3. 彼女は話すことができませんが，指とコンピューター処理技術を使ってコミュニケーションを図ることは可能です。

D **Summary Practice:** Fill in the blanks with suitable words beginning with the letters indicated. Then listen to the CD and check your answers.

DL 43 CD2-36

Attendees of this year's graduation at (1. **R**) (2. **C**) in Florida were treated to a memorable (3. **c**) speech. (4. **V**) Elizabeth Bonker, a (5. **S**) (6. **I**) major with a 4.0 average, is in fact (7. **n**). Diagnosed with a form of (8. **a**) which prevents her from speaking, Elizabeth nonetheless has learned to (9. **c**) by using her (10. **f**) to point to (11. **l**) to spell out (12. **w**). The rest is done through computer-generated (13. **t**)-to-(14. **s**) technology. In her message, the top graduate acknowledged the (15. **i**) of a non-speaking autistic urging those in the audience to use their (16. **v**) and to be the (17. **l**). She also made them realize the importance of doing things that no one can (18. **i**). Cheers to you, Elizabeth!

E **Discussion:** Share your ideas and opinions with your classmates.

1. In Elizabeth's message she briefly mentions how she as a nonverbal person and how deaf people are able to communicate with others. See if you can find more information about the communication strategies of nonverbal and deaf people.
2. In her commencement speech, Elizabeth urges her fellow graduates to "be the light." What do you think she means by that?
3. The story of Helen Keller, who was both blind and deaf, and Anne Sullivan, who taught her to communicate, is immortalized in the 1962 movie *The Miracle Worker*. If you are able to, watch the film and talk about it with your classmates.

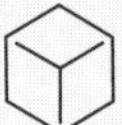

Useful Grammar from the News

vol.3

ハイフンをつけた複合形容詞

ニュース英語では簡潔な表現が好まれるため，複合形容詞が頻出する。複合形容詞とは，２語以上の単語をハイフンで結び付けた形容詞で，後続の名詞を修飾したり補語になったりする。名詞の後ろに関係代名詞節を加えて長々と説明しなければならない場面などでも，複合形容詞を使うことで簡潔に臨場感をもって説明することができる。

例えば，下記の例ではハイフンでつながれた複合形容詞が使われているため簡潔に表現されている。

—Finding her voice with ***computer-generated***, ***text-to-speech*** technology.

(*Valedictorian Speech, P.93 L.16*)

もし複合形容詞を使わなければ，“Finding her voice with speech synthesis technology that is generated by computer.”というように関係代名詞を使った説明的な文になる。

—…right here to be ***hand-stamped*** by our volunteers.

(*Volunteers in Loveland, P.10 L.14*)

—The national holiday acknowledges the ***long-fought*** freedom for black Americans living in chattel slavery. (*Commemorating Juneteenth, P.15 L.13*)

—In Ft. Worth, ***95-year-old*** Opal Lee, a leading advocate of the holiday…

(*Commemorating Juneteenth, P.15 L.19*)

—…, they have hundreds of vetted, ***shovel-ready*** projects, …

(*Colorado River Most Endangered, P.29 L.36*)

—There is now a ***64-person*** wait list for Dillon’s book.

(*An Inspiring Child Author, P.54 L.26*)

—…Remington marketed their guns to get them in the hands of impressionable, ***violent-prone*** young men… (*Historic Gunmaker Settlement, P.62 L.46*)

—And currents bring ***nutrient-rich*** cold water from Antarctica.

(*Saving the Galapagos, P.67 L.10*)

—With inflation at an ***eye-watering*** 8.5 percent, … (*Rising Prices, P.80 L.17*)

Historic Confirmation

The Gist
- Why is Ketanji Brown Jackson's confirmation considered to be historic?
- How does President Biden feel about the appointment?

Before You Watch the News — *Warm-up Exercises*

A Vocabulary Check: Choose the correct definition for each of the words below.

DL 44 CD2-37

1. potential ( ) a. to smile brightly
2. fulfill ( ) b. easily spread from one person to another
3. beam ( ) c. to achieve or realize
4. contagious ( ) d. important; meaningful
5. consequential ( ) e. qualities that may lead to future success

B Fill in the blanks with appropriate expressions from the Vocabulary Check above. Change the word forms where necessary.

1. Joann's enthusiasm is ( )! Half the students in her class volunteered to help clean the riverbank with her next weekend.
2. Sally is ( ). She must have done well in the skating competition.
3. With his brain and good study habits, Kip has the ( ) to go on to a top law school.
4. Never forget that words are ( ). Think carefully before you speak.
5. Next year my parents hope to ( ) their dream of visiting Ireland, where my grandparents were born.

Focus on the News Story

D. Muir: Here at home, tonight, and at the White House today, history made.

Judge Ketanji Brown Jackson's powerful, emotional speech. What she said, as she now becomes the first black woman to serve on the Supreme Court.

She said it took 232 years, 115 appointments for a black woman 1. ______________________________ on the Supreme Court of the United States. Here's our senior White House correspondent, Mary Bruce.

M. Bruce: Judge Ketanji Brown Jackson stepping out of the White House today and into history.

Vice President K. Harris: Today is indeed a wonderful day.

M. Bruce: Vice President Kamala Harris, 2. ______________________________ ______________________________, describing a letter she wrote to her own goddaughter moments after presiding over Jackson's Senate confirmation.

Vice President K. Harris: I told her that I felt such a deep sense of pride and joy. And I will tell you, her braids are just a little longer than yours, but as I wrote to her, I told her what I knew this would mean for her life and all that she has in terms of potential.

M. Bruce: For President Biden, a campaign promise fulfilled.

President J. Biden: This is not only a sunny day. [3.] ______________________________ ______________________________. This is gonna let so much shine, sun shine on so many young women, so many young black women.

M. Bruce: Jackson listening, beaming, and wiping away tears.

President J. Biden: You are the very definition of what we Irish refer to as dignity.

Vice President K. Harris: Yeah.

President J. Biden: You have enormous dignity. And this communicates to people, it's contagious, and it matters. It matters a lot.

M. Bruce: Then it was her turn.

K. B. Jackson, Associate Justice, US Supreme Court: It has taken 232 years and 115 prior appointments for a black woman to be selected to serve on the Supreme Court of the United States. But we've made it. We've made it, all of us. All of us. And… and [4.] ______________________________ that they see now more than ever that here, in America, anything is possible.

Vice President K. Harris: That's right.

M. Bruce: The judge thanking her husband, her two daughters, and her parents, both teachers, raised in the Jim Crow South.

K. B. Jackson: No one does this on their own. The path was cleared for me, so that I might rise to this occasion. And in the poetic words of Dr. Maya Angelou, "I do so now, while bringing the gifts my ancestors gave. I... **5.** ______________________________ ______________."

M. Bruce: Describing this as a moment all Americans should be proud of.

K. B. Jackson: We have come a long way toward perfecting our union. In my family, it took just one generation to go from segregation to the Supreme Court of the United States.

D. Muir: A really powerful day, there on the South Lawn. Mary Bruce, you were right there. And I know President Biden described the moment in his words as historic, consequential. He said **6.** __________ ______________, the people assembled today at the White House will tell their children and their grandchildren that, "I was there."

M. Bruce: David, this is a defining day for this presidency. Biden said when he decided to run, he envisioned this very moment, calling it a day of hope, promise and progress. You know, we witness a lot of history here, David, but rarely have I seen an event so joyful. Hundreds gathered here to be a part of this. Many black women who beamed along with Judge Jackson and **7.** ____________________ ____________, as well. Judge Jackson will now have a few more months before she officially ascends to the bench later this summer, after Justice Breyer retires.

Notes

L.7 **senior White House correspondent** 「ホワイトハウス担当上席記者」

L.14 **goddaughter** 「名付け娘〈キリスト教の洗礼にあたり，名付け親の立会いを受けた子のこと。キリスト教では，両親が亡くなった場合に備えて，親族や友人に子どもの面倒を見てもらう人を名付け親（godparent）として指定することがある。名付け子が娘の場合は goddaughter，息子の場合は godson と呼ばれる〉

L.14 **presiding over ~** 「～の議長を務める；～を取り仕切る」

L.15 **Senate confirmation** 「= Senate confirmation hearing 上院の（指名承認）公聴会」

L.26 **what we Irish refer to as dignity** 「われわれアイルランド人（アイルランド系アメリカ人）が言うところの「尊厳」〈バイデン大統領は，アイルランド系カトリックの中産階級の家庭の生まれで，伝統的に尊厳を重んじる〉」

L.31 **Associate Justice, US Supreme Court** 「米国連邦最高裁判事」

L.32 **prior appointments** 「先任者の任命〈1789 年の最高裁設立以来，ジャクソン氏の前に最高裁判事を務めた判事は 115 人いた〉」

L.39 **Jim Crow South** 「ジム・クロウ制のあった南部〈1870 年代以降，アメリカ南部諸州で定められた黒人に対する差別的法律の総称を Jim Crow Laws（ジム・クロウ法）と呼ぶ〉」

L.41 **Dr. Maya Angelou** 「マヤ・アンジェロウ博士〈アメリカの作家，詩人，公民権運動家として活動した黒人女性。1928-2014〉」

L.47 **segregation** 「人種隔離；人種差別」

L.49 **South Lawn** 「サウスローン；ホワイトハウス南側に面した芝生」

L.55 **defining day** 「決定的な日；画期的な日」

L.62 **ascends to the bench** 「判事として就任する」

L.63 **Justice Breyer** 「ブライヤー判事〈1994 年に民主党のクリントン大統領（当時）に指名されて以来，リベラル派として米連邦最高裁判所の判事を務めた〉」

Background of the News

連邦最高裁（the Supreme Court of the United States）の233年の歴史のなかで，初めての黒人女性判事としてケタンジ・ブラウン・ジャクソン判事（Judge Ketanji Brown Jackson）が誕生した。最高裁判事は終身制だが，2022年１月にリベラル派のブライヤー判事（Justice Breyer）が83歳で引退表明したことを受け，バイデン氏が後任を指名した。

最高裁は判事９人で構成し，トランプ前大統領が保守派３人を指名したことで保守派６人，リベラル派３人と，保守に大きく傾斜していた。ジャクソン判事もブライヤー判事と同じリベラル派と位置づけられ，保守派優勢という現在の構成割合は変わらない。現在は，ジャクソン判事以外に女性判事が３人おり，黒人男性は１人，ヒスパニック系は１人いる。

最高裁は2022年６月24日，中絶の権利を憲法上の権利と認めた1973年の「ロー対ウェード判決」（Roe v. Wade Judgement）を覆すという歴史的な判決を出した。最高裁の判決はその社会的影響力が大きく，今回の米世論を二分する判決はアメリカ社会の分断を一層深める恐れがあるといわれている。バイデン大統領はこの判決に反発し，2022年11月の大統領中間選挙では中絶の権利を争点にすることにしているという。

After You Watch the News Exercises

A Listen to the news story and fill in the blanks in the text.

B **Multiple Choice Questions:** Select the best answer to each question.

1. Ketanji Brown Jackson
   a. fulfilled one of her campaign promises today.
   b. is the child of parents who lived under segregation.
   c. tried for many years to become a Supreme Court judge.

2. Which of the following did ***NOT*** occur at the White House event?
   a. The new appointee beamed and shed tears.
   b. Brown Jackson quoted a poem written by a famous black poet.
   c. The vice president's goddaughter read a letter to Brown Jackson.

3. President Biden
   a. praised Judge Brown Jackson's ancestors in his speech.
   b. praised Judge Brown Jackson for her enormous dignity.
   c. hadn't expected to place a black woman on the Supreme Court.

4. The Supreme Court of the United States
   a. has never before appointed a female judge.
   b. has been in existence for nearly 200 years.
   c. will be joined by their new member in a few months.

C Translate the following Japanese into English. Then listen to the CD and practice the conversation with your partner.

DL 45 CD2-40

A: Do I see tears? Why are you crying, Mom?

B: These are happy tears. 1. ______________________.

A: Is it really such a big deal? There are other female judges.

B: 2. But ______________________

______________________. We should feel so proud!

A: I guess you're right. But since I was accepted at Harvard, I feel like we black women can do anything.

B: 3. ______________________

______________________.

A: You're right, Mom. This is a day of hope.

1. これはアメリカにとってとても誇らしい瞬間です。
2. でも，ケタンジ・ブラウン・ジャクソンは黒人女性として初めて最高裁判事になったのです。
3. それは，ジャクソン判事やハリス副大統領のような人たちが，あなたのために道を切り開いてくれたからです。

D **Summary Practice:** Fill in the blanks with suitable words beginning with the letters indicated. Then listen to the CD and check your answers.

DL 46 CD2-41

It was a (1. **d**) day for President Biden's (2. **p**) as Judge Ketanji Brown Jackson made (3. **h**) by becoming the first (4. **b**) (5. **w**) ever appointed to the (6. **S**) (7. **C**). In her powerful speech, Judge Jackson thanked her husband, her (8. **d**) and her (9. **p**), who both grew up in the (10. **J**) (11. **C**) (12. **S**). She also cited the words of (13. **M**) (14. **A**), saying, "I am the (15. **d**) and the hope of the (16. **s**)." In a day filled with joy and (17. **t**) of emotion, the president stressed that Ketanji Brown Jackson's appointment would let the sun (18. **s**) on many young black women. He also told the hundreds of people gathered at the (19. **W**) (20. **H**) that they would someday tell their children and grandchildren that they had been there to (21. **w**) this historical event.

E Discussion: Share your ideas and opinions with your classmates.

1. This news story was broadcast when Judge Ketanji Brown Jackson's appointment to the Supreme Court was first confirmed. Look for updates on Ketanji Brown Jackson's role on the Court.

2. Three powerful black women are mentioned in this news story: Vice President Kamala Harris, Supreme Court Judge Ketanji Brown Jackson, and renowned poet Maya Angelou. Look for information on other African American women who have made a mark on American culture.

3. How much do you know about the Supreme Court of the United States? Do an internet search to learn about the history and role of the highest Court, as well as its membership. In what ways is it similar to and different from Japan's Supreme Court?

Appendix

Map of the United

CANADA

Washington
11
Montana
North Dakota
Minnesota
Oregon
14
Idaho
South Dakota
Wyoming
Iowa
Nevada
Nebraska
1
Utah
Colorado
California
Kansas
8
7
Arizona
6
New Mexico
Oklahoma
5 18
Alaska
Texas
17
3
MEXICO
Hawaii

States

❶〜⓳はニュースに登場した都市名で，州名はイタリックになっています。各都市の位置は，地図上に番号で示しています。

News Story **1**

❶ Loveland, *Colorado*

News Story **2**

Texas

❷ Milwaukee, *Wisconsin*

❸ Galveston, *Texas*

❹ Buffalo, *New York*

❺ Ft. Worth, *Texas*

News Story **3**

❻ Scottsdale, *Arizona*

News Story **4**

Colorado

❼ Los Angeles (LA), *California*

❽ Las Vegas, *Nevada*

News Story **5**

Florida

News Story **6**

❾ Brooklyn, *New York*

❿ Pittsfield, *Massachusetts*

⓫ Portland, *Oregon*

⓬ Cambridge, *Massachusetts*

❼ Los Angeles, *California*

⓭ New York, *New York*

News Story **8**

⓮ Boise, *Idaho*

News Story **9**

⓯ Newtown, *Connecticut*

News Story **11**

⓰ Richmond, *Virginia*

⓱ Houston, *Texas*

News Story **12**

⓲ Dallas, *Texas*

News Story **14**

⓳ Winter Park, *Florida*

TVニュース英語とは

1 アメリカ国内テレビニュース英語の特徴

本書は直接ニューヨークで受信したテレビニュースから素材を選定し，米国ABC放送局本社からニュース映像を提供してもらいテキストに編集している。

ニュース英語は伝えるメディア媒体の種類上，大きく分けて３種類に分類される。第１は新聞，雑誌などに代表される活字で伝えられるもの，第２にはラジオのように音声情報に頼る媒体から提供されるもの，そして第３番目はネットやテレビを介して音声情報と画像情報が同時に供給されるニュースである。ここでは，第３番目のメディア媒体であるテレビ放送におけるニュース英語の特徴を簡単にまとめてみた。ニュース英語というと使用される英語もフォーマルなイメージがあるが，実際には以下で述べるように口語的な特徴も多く見られる。ここで引用している例文は *World News Tonight* で実際使われたものばかりである。

1.1 ニュースの構成

まず，放送スタジオにいるアンカーパーソンが，そのニュースの中心情報をリード部分で述べ，何についてのニュースであるかを視聴者に知らせる。アンカーパーソンは，ごく短くそのニュースの概要を紹介し，リポーターへとバトンタッチする。次にリポーターが現地からのリポートを，ときにはインタビューなどを交えながら詳しく報告する，というのがテレビニュースの一般的なパターンになっている。それを略図で示したのが次の図である。ひとつのニュースの放送時間は割合短く，普通1.5〜3分程度である。

●ニュースの構成

・LEAD
・INTRODUCTION（放送スタジオ）

・リポーターへの導入表現

Reporter

・MAIN BODY（現地からのリポート，インタビューなど）

・リポーターの結びの表現

1.2 比較的速いスピード

発話速度は大学入学共通テストのリスニング問題で平均毎分約130語前後，英検２級では150語前後ぐらいだといわれている。しかし，生の(authentic)英語になると，かなり発話速度が速くなる。英語母語話者が話す速度は，インフォーマルな会話の場合，平均毎分210語で，速い場合は人によって230 wpm (words per minute) になる。典型的なフォーマル・スタイルの英語である，アメリカ国内のテレビニュース放送(ABC放送)を筆者が調べたところ，発話速度は平均163〜198 wpmであることが分かった。生の英語でも一般的にフォーマルな話しことばほど発話速度は落ちてくるが，アメリカ国内用のテレビニュースは比較的速い方に分類される。

1.3 不完全文の多用

テレビニュース英語では，be動詞や主語，動詞が省略された「不完全文」が多く，端的で箇条書き的な表現が好んで使われる。例えば，以下の例はABC放送で実際に使用されていた文である。これらは散列文(loose sentence)として，書きことばでは非文とされるが，テレビニュース英語ではよく現れる不完全文の一例と考えられる。

— Gloves worn by elevator operators, ticket takers and taxi drivers.

上記を補足的に書き換えると以下のようになる。

— Gloves [were] worn by elevator operators, ticket takers and taxi drivers.

次は，シェイクスピアが人気があることを伝えるニュースからの例である。

— Four hundred years, 20 generations and still going strong.

これを，説明的に補足すれば，以下のようになる。

— Four hundred years [or] 20 generations [have passed since he died and he is] still going strong.

新聞英語の見出しではbe動詞が省略されることはよく知られているが，テレビニュース英語では，主語・一般動詞・be 動詞・関係代名詞などを省略し，箇条書き的な文体で情報を生き生きと伝える。文法より，伝達する意味内容を重視するため，短い語句をたたみかけるように次々つなぐのである。特に，ニュースの冒頭部分で何についての報道であるか，そのトピックを告げるときにこの文体はよく用いられる。以下の(∧)は，そこに何らかの項目が省略されていることを示している。

— ∧ Sixty-nine years old, ∧ married for 35 years, ∧ lives in Honolulu.

— The weather was calm, the tide ∧ high, ...

— Today, ∧ the battle for Ohio.

このような不完全文を使うことによって，ニュースに緊張感や臨場感を持たせ，視聴者の興味を引き付けている。テレビニュースの場合は視聴者の視覚に訴える画像情報があるので，完全で説明的な文体を使用するよりは，むしろ箇条書的な不完全文の方が視聴者にアピールしやすい。

1.4 現在時制が多い

最新のニュースを伝えるというテレビニュースの即時性を考えれば，現在形や近い未来を表す表現が多いことは容易に予想される。米ABC放送のニュースにおける時制について調べたところ，現在形と現在進行形で46%を占めていることが分かった。現在形や進行形の多用は臨場感を生み出す。

— The world's largest carmakers say they ***are going to*** lower the frame on sport utility vehicles...
— ..., and Rome's police ***are*** aggressively ***enforcing*** the new law, ...
— Americans now ***spend*** more time on the job than workers in any other developed country.
— ...their budget shortfalls ***are*** so severe they ***are going*** to raise taxes.
— Now AmeriCorps ***is telling*** future volunteers there may be no place for them.

新聞などの書きことばにおけるニュース英語では，未来を表すのに"be expected to"，"be scheduled to"，"be to"などやや固い表現がよく使われるが，口語的なニュース英語では"will"が好んで使用される。

— In this crowd, there are damning claims that she is being starved, that she ***will*** suffer.
— For now, some colleges ***will*** ignore scores for the new writing section, ...

1.5 伝達動詞はsayが多い

ニュース英語の特徴として「誰々がこう言った，何々によればこういうことである」といった構文が多く現れる。主語＋伝達動詞＋(that)節という構文では，伝達動詞はsayが圧倒的に多く用いられる。構文に変化を付けるために，主節が文中に挿入されたり，文尾に後置されたりする場合も多い。

— One result of higher temperatures, ***says*** the government, is more extremes in the weather, ...
— But that's the male reaction, ***say*** the researchers.

直接話法では，Mary said to Cathy, "I like your new car."というように，「発言者＋伝達動詞」が被伝達部に先行するのが一般的である。ニュースの英語では，このような直接話法を使って「…が～と言いました」という表現はよく見られるが，以下のように「発言者＋伝達動詞」が被伝達部の後に出でくる場合も多い。また，以下の冒頭例のように，発言者が人称代名詞以外の名詞であれば，伝達動詞が先に来る。

— "It turns out they're a lot more like people than we thought," ***says*** the director of the Wolong reserve.
— "I'm going to use an expression," he ***says***.
— "It's strange to be here," he ***says***.
— "Soon, we're planning to fly from Baghdad to Europe," he ***says***.

1.6 縮約形の多用

以下のような指示代名詞，人称代名詞や疑問代名詞の後のbe動詞，助動詞の縮約形(contraction)がよく使われる：it's, that's, we'll, don't, I'm, you're, here's, they're, we're, we've, can't, won't, what's.

縮約形はくだけた会話英語の特徴である。以下の例からも分かるように，テレビニュース英語では新聞英語とは異なって，縮約形の使用によりインフォーマルな雰囲気が出ている。書きことばの原稿をただ読み上げるのではなくて，視聴者にとって親しみやすい響きを与える口語的なスタイルが心がけられている。

— And the reason why, George, is ***they've*** learned that the Made in the USA tag carries real weight in China.
— ***It's*** been decades since then, but polio is still very much alive.
— Add it all up and America's happiest person ***isn't*** Tom Selleck, ***it's*** Alvin Wong.
— ..., the one that comes when you ***can't*** put down the Blackberry or iPhone at home, ...
— ***She's*** constantly juggling his needs and those of the Cincinnati ad agency she works for.

2 テレビニュースの表現

2.1 冒頭部分の特徴

ストーリーの全体を予想させたり，ニュース内容に期待を持たせたりするために，ニュースの冒頭には短いインパクトのある表現や，やや大げさな表現が置かれる。以下の例は気球に乗って初めて世界一周に成功した人のニュースである。

— ***History was made today*** above the Sahara Desert ー man, for the first time, has flown around the world nonstop in a balloon.

新聞英語では，冒頭の文(lead)で読者の注意をひきつけるために，書き方が工夫されることが多い。テレビニュース英語でも，新しいニュースの始まりの部分では疑問文，繰り返し，文法的に不完全な文などを用いて視聴者の興味をひきつけようとする。

— Finally this evening, ***not just another pretty face.***

— ***The weather, the weather, always the weather.***

— Finally, this evening, ***will they turn the panda cam back on again?***

2.2 リポーター紹介の表現

アンカーパーソンがニュースの主要情報を紹介した後，リポーターにバトンタッチするときの表現である。日本語のニュースでは「では，現場の～がリポートします」に当たる部分で，次のようにさまざまなバリエーションがある。

— And tonight, Dr. Richard Besser takes us to a remote part of the world, ...

— ABC's Abbie Boudreau is in Provo, Utah.

— It's a duel in the Capitol Hill cafeteria and Jon Karl explains.

— We asked Bianna Golodryga to find out.

— Lisa Stark explains why.

— Here's John Berman on health, wealth and birth order.

— Jim Avila is at a McDonald's in Newark, New Jersey, tonight. Jim?

アンカーパーソンが，現場のリポーターや別の放送スタジオにいるニュースキャスターを呼び出すときには，その人にファーストネームで呼びかける。呼びかけられた人は，自分の読む原稿が終了して元のアンカーパーソンに戻したいときにもまたファーストネームで呼びかける。名前の呼び合いがバトンタッチの合図にもなっている。

— **D. Sawyer**: Jim Avila is at a McDonald's in Newark, New Jersey, tonight. ***Jim?***

— **J. Avila**: Well, ***Diane,*** in this one McDonald's alone, more than 1,000 people applied for what's likely to be four jobs.

— **J. Karl**: ..., it's probably going to last in a landfill somewhere for thousands and thousands of years. ***Diane?***

— **D. Sawyer**: Okay, ***Jon.*** That was one sad spoon earlier.

2.3 リポーターの結びの表現

リポーターは現場からの報道の最後を決まりきった表現で結ぶ。リポーターの名前，放送局，リポート地が告げられる。それぞれの間にポーズを入れ，少しゆっくりめに言われるのが共通した特徴である。

— John Berman, ABC News, New York.
— Lisa Stark, ABC News, Washington.
— Barbara Pinto, ABC News, Chicago.
— Jeffrey Kofman, ABC News, Nairobi.

2.4 ニュースとニュースのつなぎ表現

ひとつのニュースから別のニュースに移行するとき，何らかのシグナルがある方が視聴者としても分かりやすい。後続のニュース内容に応じたさまざまな表現を使って新しいニュースの始まりを合図している。

— ***And finally tonight,*** what makes someone the happiest person in America?
— ***Now to a story about*** the struggle between technology and family time.
— ***And finally,*** our "Person of the Week."
— ***And now, we move on to*** an incredible scene across the country today beneath the iconic symbol of corporate America, McDonald's.
— ***Tonight,*** we want to tell you about something new in the use of brain surgery to control tremors from a number of causes.

2.5 コマーシャル前のつなぎの表現

コマーシャルの間にチャンネルを変えられないよう，次のニュースの予告をする際，以下のようにさまざまな工夫をした表現が使われる。

— And when we come back, a master class in enduring crisis from the Japanese people.
— And coming up next, what's become one of those annual rites of spring.
— When we come back here on the broadcast tonight, we switch gears and take a look at this.

2.6 番組終了時の表現

その日のニュース番組は，挨拶や次回の予告などで終わる。

— And be sure to watch "Nightline" later on tonight. Our co-anchor Bill Weir is here－right here in Japan, as well.
— And we'll see you back here from Japan tomorrow night. Until then we hope you have a good night at home in the United States.
— And that's it from us for now.

最近のTVニュースに現れた略語

■ A

AAA [Automobile Association of America] 全米自動車連盟
AARP [American Association of Retired Persons] 全米退職者協会
ABA [American Bar Association] 米国弁護士協会
ABC [American Broadcasting Companies] ABC放送
ABC [American-born Chinese] アメリカ生まれの中国人
ACA [Affordable Care Act] 医療費負担適正化法
ACLU [American Civil Liberties Union] 米国自由人権協会
ACT [American College Test] 米大学入学学力テスト
ADHD [attention-deficit hyperactivity disorder] 注意欠陥・多動性障害
AI [artificial intelligence] 人工知能
AIDS [acquired immune deficiency syndrome] 後天性免疫不全症候群
AMA [American Medical Association] 米国医師会
ANC [African National Congress] アフリカ民族会議
AOL [America Online] アメリカ・オンライン：アメリカのパソコン通信大手
AP [Associated Press] AP通信社：アメリカ最大の通信社
ASEAN [Association of Southeast Asian Nations] アセアン；東南アジア諸国連合
ATF [Federal Bureau of Alcohol, Tobacco and Firearms] アルコール･たばこ･火器局[米]
ATM [automated teller (telling) machine] 現金自動預け払い機
AT&T [American Telephone and Telegraph Corporation] 米国電話電信会社
ATV [all-terrain vehicle] オフロードカー

■ B

BART [Bay Area Rapid Transit] バート：サンフランシスコ市の通勤用高速鉄道
BBC [British Broadcasting Corporation] 英国放送協会
BSA [Boy Scouts of America] 米国ボーイ・スカウト
BYU [Brigham Young University] ブリガム・ヤング大学

■ C

CBO [Congressional Budget Office] 連邦議会予算局
CBS [Columbia Broadcasting System]（米国）コロンビア放送会社
CCTV [China Central Television] 国営中国中央テレビ
CDC [Centers for Disease Control and Prevention] 疾病対策センター［米］
CEO [chief executive officer] 最高経営役員
CHP [Department of California Highway Patrol] カリフォルニア・ハイウェイ・パトロール
CIA [Central Intelligence Agency] 中央情報局［米］
CNN [Cable News Network] シー・エヌ・エヌ
COLA [cost-of-living adjustment] 生活費調整

COO [chief operating officer] 最高執行責任者
COVID-19 [coronavirus disease 2019] 新型コロナウイルス感染症
CPSC [(U.S.) Consumer Product Safety Commission] 米消費者製品安全委員会
CT [computerized tomography] CTスキャン；コンピュータ断層撮影

■ D

DC [District of Columbia] コロンビア特別区
DHS [Department of Homeland Security] 国土安全保障省［米］
DJIA [Dow Jones Industrial Average] ダウ（ジョーンズ）工業株30種平均
DMV [Department of Motor Vehicles] 自動車局：車両登録や運転免許を扱う
DMZ [Demilitarized Zone] 非武装地帯
DNA [deoxyribonucleic acid] デオキシリボ核酸：遺伝子の本体
DNC [Democratic National Committee] 民主党全国委員会
DOD [Department of Defense] アメリカ国防総省
DOJ [Department of Justice] 司法省［米］
DPRK [Democratic People's Republic of Korea] 朝鮮民主主義人民共和国
DST [Daylight Saving Time] サマータイム；夏時間
DVD [digital versatile disc] ディーブイディー：大容量光ディスクの規格
DWI [driving while intoxicated] 酒酔い運転；酒気帯び運転

■ E

EDT [Eastern Daylight (saving) Time] 東部夏時間［米］
EEZ [exclusive economic zone] 排他的経済水域
EF-Scale [Enhanced Fujita scale] 改良（拡張）藤田スケール：竜巻の強度を表す６段階の尺度
EMS [European Monetary System] 欧州通貨制度
EPA [Environmental Protection Agency] 環境保護庁［米］
ER [emergency room] 救急処置室
ES cell [embryonic stem cell] ES細胞；胚性幹細胞：あらゆる種類の組織・臓器に分化できる細胞
EU [European Union] 欧州連合
EV [electric(al) vehicle] 電気自動車

■ F

FAA [Federal Aviation Administration] 連邦航空局［米］
FBI [Federal Bureau of Investigation] 連邦捜査局［米］
FCC [Federal Communications Commission] 連邦通信委員会［米］
FDA [Food and Drug Administration] 食品医薬品局［米］
FEMA [Federal Emergency Management Agency] 連邦緊急事態管理局［米］
FIFA [Federation of International Football Associations (Fédération Internationale de Football Association)] フィーファ；国際サッカー連盟
FRB [Federal Reserve Bank] 連邦準備銀行［米］

FRB [Federal Reserve Board] 連邦準備制度理事会［米］
FTC [Federal Trade Commission] 連邦取引委員会［米］
FWS [Fish and Wildlife Service] 魚類野生生物局［米］

■ G

G8 [the Group of Eight] 先進（主要）８カ国（首脳会議）
G-20 [the Group of Twenty (Finance Ministers and Central Bank Governors)] 主要20カ国・地域財務相・中央銀行総裁会議
GAO [General Accounting Office] 会計検査院［米］
GDP [gross domestic product] 国内総生産
GE [General Electric Company] ゼネラル・エレクトリック：アメリカの大手総合電機メーカー
GM [General Motors Corporation] ゼネラル・モーターズ社：アメリカの大手自動車メーカー
GMA [Good Morning America] グッド・モーニング・アメリカ〈ABC放送の朝の情報・ニュース番組〉
GMT [Greenwich Mean Time] グリニッジ標準時
GNP [gross national product] 国民総生産
GOP [Grand Old Party] ゴップ：アメリカ共和党の異名
GPA [grade point average] 成績平均点（値）：グレード・ポイント・アベレージ
GPS [global positioning system] 全地球測位システム

■ H

HBO [Home Box Office] ホーム・ボックス・オフィス：アメリカ最大手のペイケーブル番組供給業者
HHS [Department of Health and Human Services] 保健社会福祉省［米］
HIV [human immunodeficiency virus] ヒト免疫不全ウイルス
HMO [Health Maintenance Organization] 保健維持機構［米］
HMS [Her (His) Majesty's Ship] 英国海軍；英国海軍艦船
HRW [Human Rights Watch] ヒューマン・ライツ・ウォッチ
HSBC [Hongkong and Shanghai Banking Corporation Limited] 香港上海銀行

■ I

IBM [International Business Machines Corporation] アイ・ビー・エム
ICBM [intercontinental ballistic missile] 大陸間弾道ミサイル
ICE [Immigration and Customs Enforcement] 移民税関捜査局［米］
ICT [information and communications technology] 情報通信技術
ID [identification] 身分証明書
IDF [Israel Defense Forces] イスラエル国防軍
IMF [International Monetary Fund] 国際通貨基金
Inc. [~ Incorporated] ～会社；会社組織の；有限会社

INS [Immigration and Naturalization Service] 米国移民帰化局
IOC [International Olympic Committee] 国際オリンピック委員会
IPCC [Intergovernmental Panel on Climate Change] 気候変動に関する政府間パネル
IQ [intelligence quotient] 知能指数
IRA [Irish Republican Army] アイルランド共和軍
IRS [Internal Revenue Service] 内国歳入庁［米］
ISIS [Islamic State of Iraq and Syria] イスラム国
IUCN [International Union for Conservation of Nature (and Natural Resources)] 国際自然保護連合

■ J

JCAHO [Joint Commission on Accreditation of Healthcare Organizations] 医療施設認定合同審査会［米］
JFK [John Fitzgerald Kennedy] ケネディー：アメリカ第35代大統領

■ L

LA [Los Angeles] ロサンゼルス
LED [light-emitting diode] 発光ダイオード
LGBTQs [lesbian, gay, bisexual, transgender and queer (questioning)] 性的少数者
LLC [limited liability company] 有限責任会社
LNG [liquefied natural gas] 液化天然ガス

■ M

M&A [merger and acquisition] 企業の合併・買収
MADD [Mothers Against Drunk Driving] 酒酔い運転に反対する母親の会［米］
MERS [Middle East Respiratory Syndrome (coronavirus)] マーズコロナウイルス
MLB [Major League Baseball] メジャー・リーグ・ベースボール［米］
MMR [measles-mumps-rubella vaccine] MMRワクチン：はしか，おたふく風邪，風疹の３種混合の予防接種
MRI [magnetic resonance imaging] 磁気共鳴映像法
MVP [most valuable player] 最高殊勲選手；最優秀選手

■ N

NAFTA [North Atlantic Free Trade Area] ナフタ；北大西洋自由貿易地域
NASA [National Aeronautics and Space Administration] ナサ；航空宇宙局［米］
NASCAR [National Association for Stock Car Auto Racing] 全米自動車競争協会
NASDAQ [National Association of Securities Dealers Automated Quotations]（証券）ナスダックシステム；相場情報システム［米］
NATO [North Atlantic Treaty Organization] 北大西洋条約機構
NBA [National Basketball Association] 全米バスケットボール協会
NBC [National Broadcasting Company] NBC放送

NCAA [National Collegiate Athletic Association] 全米大学体育協会
NCIC [National Crime Information Center] 全米犯罪情報センター
NFL [National Football League] ナショナル［米プロ］・フットボール・リーグ
NGO [non-governmental organization] 非政府（間）組織；民間非営利団体
NHL [National Hockey League] 北米プロアイスホッケー・リーグ
NHTSA [National Highway Traffic Safety Administration] 幹線道路交通安全局［米］
NIH [National Institutes of Health] 国立保健研究［米］
NRA [National Rifle Association] 全米ライフル協会
NSA [National Security Agency] 国家安全保障局［米］
NTSA [National Technical Services Association] 全国輸送安全委員会［米］
NTSB [National Transportation Safety Board] 国家運輸安全委員会［米］
NV [Nevada] ネバダ州（アメリカ）
NYPD [New York City Police Department] ニューヨーク市警察

■ O

OMB [the Office of Management and Budget] 行政管理予算局
OPEC [Organization of Petroleum Exporting Countries] 石油輸出国機構

■ P

PGA [Professional Golfers' Association] プロゴルフ協会〈正式には，全米プロゴルフ協会はProfessional Golfers' Association of America（PGA of America）〉
PGD [pre-implantation genetic diagnosis] 着床前遺伝子診断
PIN [personal identification number] 暗証番号；個人識別番号
PLO [Palestine Liberation Organization] パレスチナ解放機構
POW [prisoner of war] 戦争捕虜
PPE [Personal Protective Equipment] 個人用防護
PVC [polyvinyl chloride] ポリ塩化ビニル

■ Q

QB [quarterback] クォーターバック（アメリカン・フットボール）

■ R

RAF [Royal Air Force] 英国空軍
RNC [Republican National Committee] 共和党全国委員会
ROK [Republic of Korea] 大韓民国
ROTC [Reserve Officers' Training Corps] 予備役将校訓練団［米］
RV [recreational vehicle] リクリエーション用自動車

■ S

SAM [surface-to-air missile] 地対空ミサイル
SARS [Severe Acute Respiratory Syndrome] 重症急性呼吸器症候群
SAT [Scholastic Aptitude Test] 大学進学適性試験［米］
SEC [(U.S.) Securities and Exchange Commission] 米証券取引委員会
SNS [social networking service] エスエヌエス；ソーシャル・ネットワーキング・サービス：インターネットを介して，友人や知人の輪を広げていくためのオンラインサービス
START [Strategic Arms Reduction Treaty] 戦略兵器削減条約
STD [sexually transmitted (transmissible) diseases] 性感染症
SUV [sport-utility vehicle] スポーツ・ユーティリティ・ビークル；スポーツ汎用車
SWAT [Special Weapons and Tactics] スワット；特別機動隊［米］

■ T

TB [tuberculosis] 結核
TOB [takeover bid] 株式の公開買付制度：企業の支配権を得るためにその企業の株式を買い集めること
TPP [Trans-Pacific Partnership] 環太平洋戦略的経済連携協定
TSA [Transportation Security Administration] 運輸保安局［米］

■ U

UA [United Airlines] ユナイテッド航空
UAE [United Arab Emirates] アラブ首長国連邦
UAW [United Automobile Workers] 全米自動車労働組合
UCLA [University of California at Los Angeles] カリフォルニア大学ロサンゼルス校
UK [United Kingdom (of Great Britain and Northern Ireland)] 英国；グレートブリテンおよび北部アイルランド連合王国：英国の正式名
UN [United Nations] 国際連合
UNICEF [United Nations International Children's Emergency Fund] ユニセフ；国連児童基金〈現在の名称はUnited Nations Children's Fund〉
USAF [United States Air Force] 米空軍
USC [the University of Southern California] 南カリフォルニア大学
USDA [United States Department of Agriculture] 米農務省
USGS [United States Geological Survey] 米国地質調査所
USMC [United States Marine Corps] 米国海兵隊

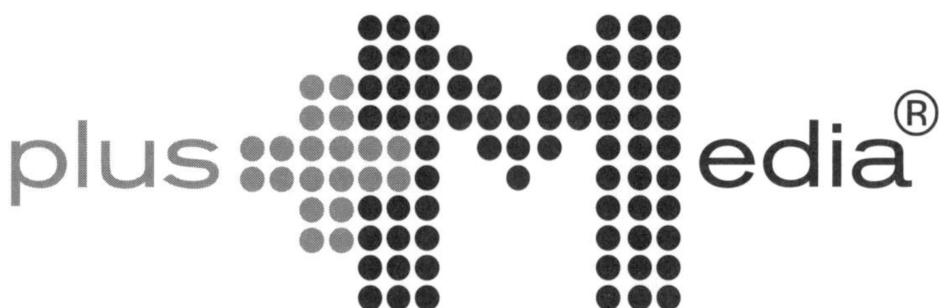

このテキストのメインページ
www.kinsei-do.co.jp/plusmedia/4171

次のページの QR コードを読み取ると直接ページにジャンプできます

オンライン映像配信サービス「plus+Media」について

本テキストの映像は plus+Media ページ（www.kinsei-do.co.jp/plusmedia）から、ストリーミング再生でご利用いただけます。手順は以下に従ってください。

ログイン

●ご利用には、ログインが必要です。
サイトのログインページ（www.kinsei-do.co.jp/plusmedia/login）へ行き、plus+Media パスワード（次のページのシールをはがしたあとに印字されている数字とアルファベット）を入力します。

●パスワードは各テキストにつき１つです。
有効期限は、はじめてログインした時点から１年間になります。

ログインページ

[利用方法]

次のページにある QR コード、もしくは plus+Media トップページ（www.kinsei-do.co.jp/plusmedia）から該当するテキストを選んで、そのテキストのメインページにジャンプしてください。

plus+Media トップ　　メインページ

メニューページ　　再生画面

「Video」「Audio」をタッチすると、それぞれのメニューページにジャンプしますので、そこから該当する項目を選べば、ストリーミングが開始されます。

[推奨環境]

iOS (iPhone, iPad)	OS: iOS 12 以降 ブラウザ：標準ブラウザ	Android	OS: Android 6 以降 ブラウザ：標準ブラウザ、Chrome
PC	OS: Windows 7/8/8.1/10, MacOS X　ブラウザ: Internet Explorer 10/11, Microsoft Edge, Firefox 48以降, Chrome 53以降, Safari		

※最新の推奨環境についてはウェブサイトをご確認ください。
※上記の推奨環境を満たしている場合でも、機種によってはご利用いただけない場合もあります。また、推奨環境は技術動向等により変更される場合があります。予めご了承ください。

このシールをはがすと
plus+Media 利用のための
パスワードが
記載されています。
一度はがすと元に戻すことは
できませんのでご注意下さい。
▼ここからはがして下さい
4171 ABC NEWSROOM
plus Media

本書には CD（別売）があります

ABC NEWSROOM
映像で学ぶ ABC放送のニュース英語

2023年１月20日　初版第１刷発行
2023年２月20日　初版第２刷発行

編著者　山根　繁
Kathleen Yamane

発行者　福岡正人
発行所　株式会社　金星堂
（〒101-0051）東京都千代田区神田神保町 3-21
Tel. (03) 3263-3828（営業部）
(03) 3263-3997（編集部）
Fax (03) 3263-0716
https://www.kinsei-do.co.jp

編集担当　四條雪菜
Printed in Japan
印刷所・製本所／大日本印刷株式会社

ISBN978-4-7647-4171-3 C1082